How to Use Your Power

OTHER NEWT LIST BOOKS
BY ERNEST HOLMES

Creative Mind

Creative Mind and Success

Ernest Holmes Speaks

Life Is What You Make It

60 Meditations for a Mindful Life

The Basics of Spiritual Mind Healing

The Bible in Light of Spiritual Philosophy

The Meaning of the Bible

The Philosophy of Emerson

The Philosophy of Jesus

The Power of This Thing Called Life

How to Use Your Power

20 Practical Lessons for Creating a Balanced Life

* * *

Ernest Holmes

newt LIST

A Newt List Publication

Chicago • New York

CONTENTS

CONTENTS

Foreword

*　　*　　*

As a Midwesterner from the "Show Me State," what I like most about Dr. Ernest Holmes' philosophy is its pragmatism. If there is a power for good in the universe, which we're immersed in and surrounded by, it makes perfect sense to learn how to use that power more effectively. We must be able to obtain specific and measurable results from our prayer work and spiritual effort. Otherwise they're either a colossal waste of time or just a salve we put on a wound to temporarily make us feel better.

In *How to Use Your Power*, Newt List has assembled twenty practical lessons from Dr. Holmes' teaching on everyday issues, such as How to Make Your Faith Real and How to Solve Your Problems. Each chapter is filled with wisdom, inspiration, and helpful tools. It can also be used as a daily spiritual practice, reading one short chapter a day and then using the meditation at the end for deeper contemplation.

What makes this book so valuable is that the reader can choose an issue they are working on, go to the pages that address that issue, and gain workable solutions and practical advice. It's like a recipe book for how to live a happier, more successful life.

Dr. Holmes famous directive to "change your thinking and change your life" has become the iconic phrase of the New Thought movement. It reminds us that any permanent or lasting change in our lives must come first from a change in our own thinking. That's why every person on the spiritual path can benefit from the use of this book. It supports a change in consciousness by inspiring the reader to think more affirmatively about themselves and the power they intrinsically possess.

Ralph Waldo Emerson said "Genius always finds itself a century too early." Though Dr. Holmes began his work in the early 1900s, perhaps now as we march forward into the 21st century we are ready for the wisdom conveyed in this powerful new book.

Dr. Chris Michaels
Author of The Power of You

*   *   *

USE THE POWER GREATER THAN YOU ARE

. . .

There is a power greater than you are, and you can use it. You are surrounded by a creative intelligence that receives the impress of your thought and acts on it. How, then, will you use this power in order that you may get the most out of life and give the most back to it?

There is a life force, an energy, and an intelligence seeking an outlet through everything. Everywhere, life is always in an active state. It is always doing something. The invisible seems to be teeming with an energy backed by an intense desire to create. We are some part of all this, and there is an irresistible desire within us to create. It doesn't matter whether it is an artist painting a canvas, a minister preaching a sermon, an actor strutting across the stage, children making mud pies, or birds building their nests. Behind everything, there is an irresistible urge to create, to express life.

There is an emotional craving for self-expression in everything. The hen wants to lay an egg and sit on it, the egg wants to produce a chicken, and the chicken wants to lay another egg and produce more chickens. The seed wants to multiply itself. It wants to become a tree in which birds will roost. The birds want to build their nests in the tree and hatch out their young. The lion, the wolf, the dog, you and I, and everything in nature have an irresistible desire and impulsion to create.

Joseph Strauss built some of the biggest objects in the world, yet he was of small physical stature. As a young boy, he couldn't play football or compete in athletics, so he made up his mind that he would someday build the biggest objects that had ever been built by human beings. The Golden Gate Bridge is a testimony not only to his engineering skills and his technical knowledge, but to the emotional craving he had to create.

One of the leading radio entertainers of our day was brought up in the country of a Midwestern state. She just couldn't help writing songs and singing them. She never had any technical training, but she had an irresistible urge to express herself, and she just kept right on doing the thing she knew how to do. Finally, she was introduced to spiritual ideas and came to realize that the thing that was working through her was a universal force. It was something bigger than she was, but it was intimate and close to her. It was real to her thought and feeling and imagination. Today she sings to the world, and everyone loves it.

Where does all this come from? The Bible says there is a river of life that flows through everything. Both Henry Ford and Thomas Edison believed that we are surrounded by divine ideas, as though the very air around us was filled with them, and they believed that these ideas were pressing against them, seeking self-expression. They followed the impulsion of these ideas and produced what seemed impossible.

Charles Schwab, the great steel master, believed this. At one time, he purchased fifty thousand copies of a book that dealt with this subject and gave them to his employees. He wanted to stimulate the feeling in them that they were backed up by a power greater than they were, and that they could use it.

Mahatma Gandhi said that there is a soul force in the universe, which, if we permit it, will flow through us and produce miraculous results. People used to call him a dreamer, an impossible idealist, but history will put him down as perhaps second to Jesus in the use of spiritual power.

There is no use in spending our time just talking about great and wonderful people, because you and I are unique individuals, and no one else can live our lives for us. Lives of great people should remind us that we, too, are great, because what can be more wonderful than that which God has created? Otherwise, of what interest could it be to us?

Too often we have thought that God crowned only a few people with glory and honor. But Jesus talked to the multitudes. He didn't feel that his words of wisdom would be lost on the average, common people who heard him so gladly. Quite the reverse, because it was Jesus who said, "Creator, I thank you that you have hid these things from the wise and the prudent, and have revealed them unto babes." Jesus knew what you and I must find out, that every person is an individual in the one Creative Mind and that everyone may draw on this Mind's intelligence, its power, and its energy. All people are rulers in their own right.

But an example is no good unless it is followed, and it will not do us a bit of good to know that there is a power greater than we are unless we use it. It isn't enough just to affirm that faith can do anything, and it is not an effective prayer merely to state that God is all there is. Of course God is all there is. Of course there is a power greater than we are, or we wouldn't be here.

If faith can produce wonderful results, then faith is something we ought to develop. If prayer and meditation can make the divine presence real to us, then we ought to pray and we ought to meditate and we ought to commune with the divine presence until it does become real to us.

It is wonderful to know that there are millions of people in our country who are making an effort to prove that there is a spiritual power that can be used for definite purposes. There is plenty of evidence that this power is being used and that it is actually producing results. You can hardly pick up a magazine or newspaper today without finding some reference to this power.

But how seldom do any of these articles analyze the meaning of faith and tell us just what it is and show us exactly how to use it? It is as though we had hit upon a new energy but don't know how it works and haven't developed techniques for its use. We are always talking about it yet never quite coming to the point where it becomes the guiding star of all our lives, a light that shines in the darkness, a rock in a weary land, an oasis in a desert. And how we need the shadow of that rock! We all need to drink from this oasis so that our desert, too, will blossom as the rose.

This power already exists at the center of our own being. It isn't something we go in search after. It isn't hid in a deep cavern. It isn't lost in the desert. It isn't obscured by the clouds that cover the lofty Alps, only occasionally showing its grandeur to our admiring gaze. This power is within us now, and more than anything else—more than all other things—we need to recognize it, because we are a seed of the divine life deposited on earth so that we will live and love and create and be happy, and that we will unite with others in the joy of knowing that the realm of heaven is on earth.

Suppose we accept this challenge and make up our minds to prove that life has not left us alone to buffet our way through the vicissitudes of fortune, mere pawns on the checkerboard of chance. First of all, we must believe in the power. We must believe that it is right where we are. We must understand that it is a power for good, and we must realize that this power flows through us, and that the instrument of this power is our own mind. We must begin right where we are, because there is no other place we could begin.

. . .

Meditation

Today I accept the presence of this power greater than I am. Today I believe that it is operating in all my affairs. Today I accept that there is a divine guidance telling me what to do. Today I affirm that there is a power that goes before me and prepares the way. I affirm that this power is love and life. I affirm that the divine presence is a presence of joy and happiness. I affirm that there is something within me that knows what to do under every circumstance and in every situation. I deliberately turn from everything that seems confusing and no longer listen to that which denies the reality of God in my experience. I allow, I believe, and I permit. I believe and I allow. I accept and I know.

HAVE SECURITY

· · ·

Why do we so often have a sense of impending disaster, and why is so much of our time spent in wondering what is going to happen in the future, until our very present is robbed of all peace of mind and we do not even sleep well at night? Let us approach this subject from three viewpoints: the physical, the mental, and the spiritual.

We do have a physical body and a physical environment, and we need proper physical care. We must have clothes to wear, food to eat, and a place in which to live. It truly is necessary that our physical requirements should be met.

But there is another kind of security we are in need of, which is psychological. This means that we have a sense of well-being inside ourselves through proper adjustment to life and to living. A vast amount of research has been carried on during the last twenty-five years in this field, and a course has been charted which, if followed, will help to give all of us an emotional security, a mental poise, and balance that will better fit us to live.

One of the interesting things in this exploration is that researchers have been able to trace much of our feeling of insecurity to early childhood, when we were being conditioned for what was going to happen to us in the future. They have discovered that the infant who feels itself to be a part of the family life in love and in confidence and in faith will generally grow up to be a self-reliant person, one who is poised and balanced and who quickly adjusts to living. They have also discovered that a sense of insecurity comes from frustrations, probably from early childhood, which are based on a feeling of not being wanted, needed, and loved.

The first law of our emotional life seems to be that we must feel wanted, needed, and loved, that we are an important part of the whole family set-up. When for any reason we feel unwanted, unneeded, and unloved, we have an unconscious sense of rejection. The mind is a funny thing, and it can operate against us as well as for us. If we feel unwanted, unloved, and unneeded, then we feel rejected, and because of this, in some peculiar way, we have an unconscious sense of guilt.

The feeling mind does not reason logically; it simply feels. The insecurity of not being wanted creates an unconscious sense of rejection and guilt, and the mind enters into a conflict with itself, as though it were trying to figure out what is wrong. It has a sense of uneasiness, and this produces a feeling insecurity and confusion. It is this inward conflict over the feeling of insecurity that creates most of the tensions and strains that go with what is called our inferiority and superiority complexes.

A feeling of inferiority robs people of hope and enthusiasm and the zest for living. It makes them feel that everything and everyone is against them and that they are contending with uneven odds for the right to live. In certain cases, this sense of inferiority creates what has been called a superiority complex, which causes people to assume an unnatural aggressiveness toward life and feel that they have to go out and knock everything over. These people are over-argumentative and sometimes disagreeable. Yet if you examine the way they think, you will discover that all this aggressiveness is built up to hide a hidden wound.

We must understand this because both the sense of being inferior and that of being superior are false. They are both created out of the illusion that we do not belong to life, that we are not a part of it, that we have been rejected by it. So we go blustering along not knowing which way to turn, driven as it were by inward forces and conflicts until we are torn apart emotionally. It is only a short step from here to physical disintegration, because our thoughts and particularly our emotions do affect our bodies. This we cannot help; it is a law of nature.

Let's examine this mind of ours, the very mind that has torn us apart, the mind that has had thoughts of insecurity and frustrations, the mind that contains all our conflicts. What is this mind other than an instrument on which thought plays some kind of a tune? It is evident that this is so because we can change our thoughts. We can remold our thinking, we can stop being confused, and we can re-adjust our mental and emotional lives to new patterns.

We have noticed in the last few years that an ever-increasing number of people in the fields of psychology and physics are insisting that we spend more time trying to develop the spiritual person, and they are right. The next great research will be in the realm of spiritual things. This is the field that you and I are interested in, because we feel that there is something lacking, something lost beyond our present horizons that we haven't discovered.

I think we should begin our investigation in a simple and direct manner. You and I were born into this world without any volition of our own. When we arrived, we had a physical body. Nature had provided this. The average baby born into this world comes with a good physical body; anything else is an exception to the rule. This body had already been planned by a divine architect who designed it with intention, and this body had everything necessary for its own evolution. The laws of its being worked automatically.

We were also born with a mind to think and a will to do. But so impressionable was this mind, so susceptible to outside influence, that very early it began to take on the conditions of those around it and early in life became conditioned for what was to happen in the future.

We were born with a body and we were born with a mind, but we were also born with something else, which is the spiritual element within us. We were born with the capacity to understand the way the body works and to find out how the mind works. The very fact that we have this capacity proves that both the body and the mind as we ordinarily understand them do have another factor, and a transcendent one, which is the Spirit.

The trouble with us up until now is that we haven't recognized this spiritual factor within us. We haven't realized that just as there are physical and mental laws, there are also spiritual laws, and that both the physical and the mental must be—and are—dominated by the spiritual. We will never be whole until we adjust our lives and our way of thinking to the realization that we are living in a spiritual universe right now.

This is why Jesus said, "Behold, the realm of God is at hand." And he meant exactly what he said. The realm of the physical is at hand, and the realm of the mental is at hand. We know this and understand it. Yet Jesus added another realm to this. He said that the realm of God is also at hand, and if you let it, it will dominate everything else. It will control everything else, and it will control it in harmony and happiness and for the well-being of the individual and the well-being of the whole human race.

We have possessed the physical realm and misused it because we didn't know any better. We have possessed the mental, emotional, and intellectual realms and misused them because of ignorance. We haven't found anything in either the physical or the mental realms that can properly govern or control themselves. This is what is wrong with the world today.

Remember, no one can really feel happy unless they feel secure. No one can be at peace in their own mind if they are harboring negative mental attitudes of fear and doubt, or malice or hatred. No one can be free from anxiety unless something greater takes its place: faith, confidence, and assurance. No one can be happy unless they are whole, and no one can be whole unless they know that they are rooted in God.

If we can come to feel that our lives are rooted in the Divine Spirit, that our minds and bodies are instruments of Spirit, that our whole experience may become the movement of this Spirit through us in our thoughts and actions, then we will begin to feel safe.

Just as surely as we do this, ninety percent of our confusions will disappear without our paying any particular attention to them. We will find that our circulation, both physically and mentally, readjusts itself to a new harmony. Our heartbeat will become part of the rhythm of the universe. Our digestive process will assimilate the food we take into the body, because the mind is assimilating the thoughts of love and peace and joy that it is fed on. We will find that we are sleeping at night and resting. We will sleep in peace and wake in joy and live in a consciousness of good.

And another miracle will take place. We will find we are one with all people. We are no longer afraid of them. We will no longer be morbidly wondering what others are thinking about us. We will become unified with them. There will not be any false aggressiveness in this. It will be just a flowing along with life easily and peacefully and happily. Out of this will come every other adjustment that is necessary, because when enough people begin to live as though God were acting through them, everyone will wish the good of others.

In such degree as we adjust to an acceptance of the Spirit flowing through us, everything in our lives will prosper. It will be as though we were gradually led of the Spirit to much and more, and there will come to us an inward serenity and peace and calm, a sense of security, a feeling of well-being such as we have never known before.

· · ·

Meditation

The law of good is flowing through me. I am one with the rhythm of life. There is nothing to be afraid of. There is nothing to be uncertain about. God is over all, in all and through all. God is right where I am. I am at peace with the world in which I live. I am at home with the Divine Spirit in which I am immersed.

How to

IMPROVE YOUR PERSONALITY

. . .

Consciousness, or the ability to know, is the most important thing in your life. It is This Thing Called Life in you acting as an individual, a person. But there is more to it than this, because you didn't create your own consciousness. It came with you when you entered this world. Consciousness, or the thing that you really are, is the gift of life. It is God in you.

You may ask, "What has all this to do with my personality?" You may say, "I want a dynamic personality. I want to be somebody. I want lovableness and charm. I want to be creative." Of course you do. It wouldn't be natural for you to feel otherwise. But what is this thing you call *myself*, this thing your friends call *you*, the person that you are, this thing that makes you different from all others and that endears you to others? It is This Thing Called Life in you. And you didn't put it there.

Walt Whitman said there is more to a person than is contained between their head and their bootstraps. Jesus, the beautiful and wise, said, "I have meat to eat that you know not of." It is this hidden source of your being that you are looking for, this high gift of heaven, this thing in you that can mold and make your personality. This is your treasure of life. This is the source of your inspiration.

There are hidden powers, undeveloped resources, unimaginable depths to your being that you can penetrate and bring to the surface. You can make your personality anything you wish it to be. But first you must come to know what you really are and who you really are.

You are God's good person, and you alone can decide whether your personality will be happy and whole, dynamic and creative, attractive or repulsive. You alone hold the golden key to a larger life. You hold it in your hand, but you cannot use this key until you first consciously connect yourself with that "something" greater than you are. This doesn't mean that you are going to get lost or become submerged in a dream or a fantasy. It means that you are going to learn to live and think and act from the feeling that there is a limitless power behind everything you do—a power for good.

Somewhere in you is the same imagination that wrote

every book ever written, the same creative genius who invented everything that makes modern life comfortable, the great artist who painted all the pictures, the composer who wrote all the songs. The very dance of life itself is in everything God ever made, and it is in you.

You may ask, "How am I going to bring all this out? How am I going to bring it to the surface? How am I going to become that wonderful, dynamic personality that I would like to be?" Perhaps the best way to begin is not to try to be so wonderful or so dynamic. Don't strain. Don't wear a mask. Don't try to be anyone but yourself. All imitation is suicide. You are you, and you are real. Coming to know the real you is not so much something you develop or create or compel as it is something you discover.

Your first step, then, is as simple as this: Hook up your personality, your physical body, your environment, and everything you do, say, and think with what you really are—an individual living in pure Spirit here and now.

God didn't make a mistake when God created you, when God implanted God's own being in your life and breathed into you the breath of life itself. God made you to be happy and whole, complete and contented. You may start, then, by believing that at the center of your being there is a real person, a lovable person, a creative person. This should not be done with conceit or arrogance, but with the utmost simplicity. You must become acquainted with yourself. You must come to know that the real you is lovable, kind, happy, and whole, and of course you can't do this unless you believe the same thing about everyone else.

This is going to contradict a lot of experience. But so does every great discovery and so does every advance in science. Who ever thought that nylon stockings could be made out of coal and water and air, or whatever else goes into them? Who thought that out of these natural resources this marvelous nylon thread could be spun into so much that goes into industry today? You may be certain that whoever thought of it contradicted everything that had gone before. You may be sure that before it was ever formed, somebody's imagination conceived its possibility, and you may be sure that the inventor who conceived its possibility was listening to something in the universe and hearing it and following its direction.

You will soon discover that thoughts of love drawn from your innermost self will make you a lovable personality. You may be sure that the image of yourself in the mirror is a projection of your own thoughts. All that it is or has or does, all the power it possesses, you give to it, and what it lacks, you withdraw from it. You may be sure that if you become calm and poised inside, everything you do will be orderly; that if you love others, they will come to love you; that if you identify yourself with success, you will become successful. And you may be sure that if you find peace in your own soul, you will be bringing peace from heaven to your environment.

Could you ask for more? Could you expect anything better? Could even God, in all God's infinite love and wisdom, have done better for you? I don't think so. The most wonderful thing about it all is that you really don't have to create this terrific personality people talk about. You don't have to influence others, as one so often thinks one must. All you have to do is to live from yourself, to express something that even you didn't create and even you couldn't destroy, something that you can and should use.

We are all cradled in the Infinite. We are all offspring of the Most High. There is in each one of us a deep yearning, a great need for a sense of security and peace, and there is also in all of us—in you, in me, in everyone who ever lived—a feeling that there is an answer to all the demands we make on life. As surely as I believe that you live, so surely I believe there is a depth and meaning to your nature that neither you nor I nor anyone else has ever fathomed—an inexhaustible resource, a perennial fountain of life, and a person that surpasses in grandeur, in beauty, and in love anything you have ever dreamed of.

. . .

Meditation

There is a key to right living, and this key is prayer—affirmative prayer. Prayer is our direct line of communion with God. Through affirmative prayer, we learn to clear the mind of negative thoughts, of doubt and fear. This we must do if we are to become aware of the presence of God within and around us.

Take as your prayer for today the following: "Know you not that you are the temple of the living God?" Join in affirming God's presence here and now. Shut every other thought out of your mind, all the distractions of the moment—the doorbell, the telephone—as you listen confidently, peacefully, quietly.

We live because life lives in us. We move because there is a universal energy activating us. We think because there is a Universal Mind thinking through us. We exist because the Spirit has seen fit to give us life. God never makes mistakes. This is why each one of us is the temple of the living God. There is a divine spark in everyone.

.

Knowing that I am one with God, and recognizing that all people live and move and have their being in that one Spirit, which is God, I know that I am one with every person I meet. Knowing that love must be at the root of all reality, I feel a deep affection for everyone I meet. Forgiving myself for all mistakes I ever have made and forgiving all others, I meet people in the simplicity of faith, in the harmony of peace, and in the joy of living.

I sincerely believe that there is a divine presence and a law of good that attracts every person and every thing to me, that belongs to me, and that, flowing through me, reaches out to everything in my life with love, with consideration, in joy and gladness.

I am learning to salute God in everyone. I meet people naturally, spontaneously, and happily. It is my desire that everyone I meet will be blessed, will feel the warmth and color and friendship that I have for the whole world. I rest in this blessed assurance that we are all one in God.

MAKE YOUR FAITH REAL

. . .

It is only because God is in us that we exist. It was to this God within that Jesus prayed when he said, "Our Creator, which art in heaven, hallowed be thy name." We are surrounded by this divine presence and it is in us.

We are also surrounded by a law of good that receives the impress of our thought and acts on it. When Jesus said, "It is done unto you as you believe," he was implying that there is a law that acts on our belief, or our faith or confidence in it. He also said that it acts on our belief in the way we believe, which is why he said, "It is done unto you as you believe."

There are two great realities with which we deal: the divine being as a living, loving presence; and a law of good which reacts to our faith or belief and which, being a law, must of necessity react to us exactly as we believe. We wish to use this law so definitely that we may know that we have a silent partner in life, something that is all-powerful, something that is for us and never against us, something that will respond in what we call the little things as well as in what we call the big things. This is why Jesus told us that not even a sparrow falls to the ground but that God knows about it.

Jesus used this power for everything. He used it to turn the water into wine, to multiply the loaves and fish, to heal the sick and raise the dead. Moreover, Jesus actually said, "What things soever you desire when you pray, believe that you receive them, and you shall have them." And Jesus meant exactly what he said.

We are not to think of things, then, as big or little, as hard or easy, and we are not to feel that the Divine Will wishes us to have only a little good or only certain types of experiences. The Divine wishes us to have everything that makes life full and happy, and there is nothing wrong with using the law of good for our purposes, provided these purposes are constructive.

Our prayers, to be effective, must be affirmations that are so formulated in the mind as to produce the actual inner acceptance of the desires expressed. It is as simple as this, and perhaps it is its very simplicity that eludes us. We must actually bring the mind to accept the good it desires even before it has experienced that particular good. Just as we would have to plant a melon seed before the law of nature can produce melons for us, in this same sense we are planting our desires in the garden of a creative law of good, which produces a plant exactly like the seed and never something else.

Therefore, when we come to use this law of good for definite purposes, we must keep the thought clear that there is something that operates on our thinking exactly as we think it, something that knows how to bring everything together in a right way, and something that is ready and willing to react.

This calls for practice and patience and a sort of good-natured flexibility, because we don't always keep our thoughts straight. But when we know that we are working with a definite principle, then we have the courage to go on and continue until finally our thoughts do become affirmative. This is what is meant by scientific prayer. This is what is meant by what we call right mental or spiritual practice. This is what we mean by using the Science of Mind philosophy consciously and for definite purposes.

Let us take a simple instance and illustrate how this would work out in actual experience. Let's take a very common occurrence in the life of so many people who believe that no one cares for them. In this instance, we will imagine that you may feel isolated and alone, and that this has gone on for a good many years. It has become a pretty solid pattern of thought in your mind. Both consciously and subconsciously, you are affirming, "I have no friends. There is something wrong with me. I am pretty much alone in the world." Because of this, you set up something of an unconscious antagonism toward others. You do this to keep your own feelings from being hurt, because your are very sensitive.

Now let's begin to re-educate your mind, or way of thinking, and let's start out by understanding that there is one divine and universal presence in which you live and move and have your being. This is God. The same presence is in everything and everyone you will ever meet. In this divine Spirit, you are already one with everyone.

But because you have been consciously and unconsciously denying this, it may take a little time to change your patterns of thought, to break down the old patterns that have denied you the privilege of enjoying others and being loved by them. So we start with this simple proposition: "God is one. God is in everyone. God is everywhere. God is in me, and the God in me goes forth with joy to meet the God in others."

Now you are actually beginning to use the Science of Mind for a definite purpose. You have a definite goal in mind, and you are going to rearrange your thinking to meet this new idea, that there is that within you which goes out in love and good companionship to all other people and returns again to you.

Whenever the thought comes up that "people don't like me" or "I haven't got that particular thing that draws others to me," you flatly deny this. You say, "I am one with all people. There is that within me which attracts every good thing into my life."

At first this may sound unreal to you because of your previous experience. But you are working on a deep conviction, a new understanding of life, something that includes everything. So you affirm, "Wherever I go, I will be met with love and interest and good camaraderie. The Spirit within me does unify with the Spirit in all people." You learn to overlook everything else.

If you seem to be met with a rebuff or something happens to discourage you, you go right back to this fundamental proposition. Patiently, with deep conviction, you say, "But there is only one God. There is one life. That life is in everyone. That life is in me. I am meeting that life in others."

Just as surely as you do this, things will begin to happen. You will find your circle of friendship beginning to extend and increase and multiply. If you practice persistently, the time will come when you no longer, either consciously or unconsciously, entertain the idea of being separated from others. You will know that you belong to life and life belongs to you.

Now let's carry this a little further. Say to yourself every day, "I am expecting new things to happen to me. I am expecting to meet new and interesting people. I am expecting an increase of good in everything I do."

Just keep right on saying this no matter what happens. Try to believe it deeply, and if any doubt comes into your mind, go right back to the fundamental thought again: "God is one. Life is one. I am some part of that life. It belongs to me and I belong to it." Go right back to this basic thought and formulate your prayers on your communion with the invisible, affirmatively causing your mind to actually accept new experiences whether you see them or not.

In doing this, you will be following the teaching of Jesus when he said that when you pray, you should go into the closet of your mind and make known your requests, or ask your Creator who sees in secret. Ask affirmatively and accept the answer in your own thought, and your Creator will reward you openly and will bring these new conditions into your experience.

Here is where you must keep faith with yourself, with the divine presence within you, and with the law of good that is operating on your thought. This law has no choice but to operate exactly as you think, and if in your mind you are delaying the activity of good, saying maybe it will happen by and by, you are actually keeping it away from you.

The process is so simple that is seems almost impossible that so much good can come out of it. But it can, and you are the only one who can ever prove it to yourself. Just as no one can live for you, so no one can think for you. Make up your mind right here and now to think for yourself. When you get right down to it, this is making God real.

. . .

Meditation

Everything that I think, say, or do is governed by divine intelligence and inspired by divine wisdom. I am guided into right action. I have confidence in myself because I have confidence in God. I am sure of myself because I am sure of God. I am aware of my partnership with the Infinite. I know that everything I do will prosper.

How to
GIVE A SPIRITUAL
PRAYER TREATMENT

. . .

Take definite time at least twice each day to be alone, to sit down and compose your mind and think about God. Try to arrive at a deep sense of peace and calm. Then assume an attitude of faith in a power greater than you are.

Next, say, "The words I speak are my law of good, and they will produce the desired result because they are operated on by a power greater than I am. Good alone goes from me, and good alone returns to me."

You are now ready to give a specific prayer treatment for yourself. Begin by saying, "This word is for myself. Everything I say is for me and about me. It is the truth about my real self." At this time, you are thinking about your spiritual nature, the divine reality of yourself, the God in you. Say, "There is one life. That life is God. That life is perfect. That life is my life now." Say this slowly and with deep meaning.

Next, say, "My body is a manifestation of the living Spirit. It is created and sustained by the one presence and the one power. That power is flowing in and through me now, animating every organ, every action, and every function of my physical being. There is perfect circulation, perfect assimilation, and perfect elimination. There is no congestion, no confusion, and no inaction. I am one with the infinite rhythm of life that flows through me in love, in harmony, and in peace. There is no fear, no doubt, and no uncertainty in my mind. I am letting the life that is perfect flow through me. It is my life now. There is one life. That life is God. That life is perfect. That life is my life now."

Now, deny everything that contradicts this. Follow each denial with a direct affirmation of its opposite. In a certain sense, you are presenting a logical argument to your own mind based on the belief that there is only one life that is perfect, and this is your life now. The evidence that you bring out in your argument should reach a conclusion that causes your own mind to accept the verdict of perfection. Remember, you are not talking about your physical body as though it were separate from the Spirit, but about God in you. Therefore, you will have no difficulty in convincing yourself that this God in you is perfect.

You have now reached a place of realization where you

enter into a feeling of assurance that comes from a consciousness of the divine presence in, around, and through you. This period of realization should last for several moments, during which you sit quietly accepting the meaning of what you have said.

Finally, say, "It is now done. It is now complete. It is now perfect. There is one life. That life is God. That life is perfect. That life is my life now."

Between these periods of meditation, try to keep your mind poised in such a way that you do not contradict what you have said in your treatment. Keep your mind open at all times to an influx of new inspiration, new power, and new life. Accept what you have said with joy and gratitude.

. . .

Meditation

In praying for specific conditions, use the following affirmations, selecting those paragraphs which apply to your need. When praying for another person, say, "This word is for [the person's name]" and then continue exactly as though you were praying for yourself.

.

Everything that I do, say, or think is governed by divine intelligence and inspired by divine wisdom. I am guided into right action. I am surrounded with friendship, love, and beauty. Enthusiastic joy, vitality, and inspiration are in everything I do. I am conscious of divine guidance, of complete happiness, abundant health, and increasing prosperity. I am aware of my partnership with the Infinite. I know that everything I do will prosper.

.

Every thought of not being wanted or of being afraid, every thought of uncertainty and doubt, is cast out of my mind. My memory goes back to God alone, in whom I live, move, and have my being. A complete sense of happiness, peace, and certainty floods me with light. I have confidence in myself because I have confidence in God. I am sure of myself because I am sure of God.

.

The Spirit within me knows the answer to the problem that confronts me. I know that the answer is here and now. It is within my own mind because God is right where I am. I now turn from the problem to the Spirit, accepting the answer. In calm confidence, in perfect trust, in abiding faith and with complete peace, I let go of the problem and receive the answer.

.

I know exactly what to do in every situation. Every idea necessary to successful living is brought to my attention. The doorway to ever-increasing opportunities for self-expression is open before me. I am continually meeting new and larger experiences. Every day brings some greater good. Every day brings more blessing and greater self-expression. I am prospered in everything I do. There is no deferment, no delay, no obstruction or obstacle, nothing to impede the progress of right action.

I identify myself with abundance. I surrender all fear and doubt. I let go of all uncertainty. I know there is no confusion, no lack of confidence. I know that what is mine will claim me, know me, and rush to me. The presence of God is with me. The mind of God is my mind. The freedom of God is my freedom. The power of God is my power.

Today I bestow the essence of love on everything. Everyone I meet will be lovely to me. My soul meets the soul of the universe in everyone. This love is a healing power touching everything into wholeness.

The law of good is flowing through me. I am one with the rhythm of life. There is nothing to be afraid of. There is nothing to be uncertain about. God is over all, in all, and through all. God is right where I am. I am at peace with the world in which I live. I am at home with the divine Spirit in which I am immersed.

How to STOP WORRYING

. . .

Wouldn't it be wonderful if we could learn to stop worrying? You and I know how futile it is to fuss and fret. Nine times out of ten, when we ask ourselves why are we so worked up, we can't put our finger on any definite reason or incident in our lives that started a worry pattern of thought. Why, then, do we worry?

Jesus said, "Take no anxious thought for the morrow." He then added that there is a truth that can set you free from the need to worry about anything.

Modern science and our new religious outlook are doing more to help us overcome our worries today than ever before. Science is showing us why we worry, and religion is teaching us why we do not have to worry. This should mean a great deal to us, because everyone worries about something. At the same time that everyone worries about something, very few people understand what worry is or how it works.

Most people have no idea what causes their worries. For example, a friend of mine who is an accomplished architect was asked to do a drawing for a new building. She is a person of experience and achievement, but when assigned to this new job, she began to worry about it. When she realized that she had become anxious, she stopped and reasoned with herself, pointing out to herself that this job is not unlike others that she has done successfully. She has a good background of training and has had years of successful experience. Technically and professionally, she is sure of herself. But still she worried.

A salesperson came to me regarding an upcoming appointment with a client. He was anxious about the meeting. He said, "I have a product to sell in which I have the greatest confidence. The person that I am meeting is not unlike other clients to whom I have spoken. I know how to present my ideas with ease, but still I am worried."

In these illustrations, this important factor is revealed: There is no apparent reason why these people should be worried, or, if there is a reason, they are unconscious of it. This leads to the important conclusion that most of the things we are worried about have no relationship to the worrying.

In the case of the architect, the assignment of the new job and the fact that she was anxious about it must stand as two separate things if we are to understand the nature of her worry and arrive at a place where she can overcome it. She must understand that these two factors have no relationship to her worry. Therefore, we are led to the conclusion that anxiety is rarely related to what we are now doing, but arises out of certain mental tendencies of which we are not aware.

The question then arises, where does worry come from and how did it get here in the first place? Let's see what psychology has to offer to explain where our worries come from. It is broadly agreed that worry is a thought pattern. We can all understand this because we are acquainted with patterns, whether they are patterns for baking a cake or building a house.

Psychology also tells us that these anxiety thought patterns were acquired either in infancy or in early childhood. Usually they were imposed on us by well-meaning but poorly informed adults through such simple ways as saying, "You can't do that," "You're a bad person," "You're no good," and so on. These statements of rejection and condemnation were repeated so many times that the infant mind accepted them as the truth about itself, and this negative idea became, by way of illustration, like a stained glass window through which the rays of light are to be filtered and conditioned throughout the rest of the child's life unless the negative thought patterns are dissolved.

Today, when you and I worry, it is because we are seeing a present situation that is colored by the mental stained glass window of many years ago. In other words, because worry or anxiety thought patterns exist within us, we attach them to the conditions at hand. Actually, since worry is an inner condition, the architect, if she had not had a new assignment about which to worry, would have found something else to attach her inner condition of anxiety to. It is like a monotonous tune being played over and over again in her mind, and one from which she can't seem to free herself.

But we now know that these worry patterns can be healed. There is greater hope for the anxious heart today than there ever has been before in the history of humankind. We should not accept this lightly. It is important that each of us overcome our anxieties and fears, because they are undesirable companions. They are enemies that strike in two devastating ways.

Anxiety attacks our body as well as our mind. Behind most cases of high blood pressure and heart disease is an insistent worry and anxiety. It is interesting to see how this works. When we begin to express our anxiety, our muscles contract. When our muscles contract, less space is provided for the flow of blood and the blood vessels become crowded. When this happens, the heart must work harder to pump the blood through the circulatory system. This overworks the heart, strains it, and may cause damage that can end in a heart attack.

If, on the other hand, anxiety expresses itself in our mental activities rather than in our physical body, we see a crippling of our mental attitudes. These people become what are called *defeatists*. They become fearful of the most normal situations in life. They frequently lose control of their emotions and thoughts concerning the simplest activities. This, carried to an extreme degree, is what is called an anxiety neurosis.

Most of us are not concerned with an anxiety that has grown to the place where it has crippled our bodies or our minds, but all of us are concerned with the garden-variety of anxiety that torments us in little ways in our everyday activities. Let's do something about it right now, and let our healing begin by looking at a mental principle that all too often has been ignored.

In infancy, an anxiety pattern was established in the subconscious. The fact that it was established is not nearly as important as the fact that it *could* be. There is nothing in the subconscious mind that hasn't been put there, and consequently there is nothing there that cannot be changed. Even though we put it there unconsciously and didn't know we were doing it, we can consciously remove it.

It is important for us to remember that there is always a subconscious reaction to our thoughts. Our unconscious mind can be thought of simply as a receptacle, a vessel into which we pour our thoughts, our dreams, our desires, and our feelings. All of these thoughts fall like snowflakes into the subconscious and hold their patterns on the face of the mirror of Mind. In all our thinking, we are making patterns on the mirror of life. These patterns condition our activities and thoughts until the patterns themselves are changed.

This offers a challenge to each of us. It makes us careful of our thoughts. It shows us the importance of directing our thoughts in such a manner as to put a new kind of pattern on life's mirror, a new kind of tendency in our subconscious mind. Our mind is like a mirror reflecting outwardly those things that are dominant in our thoughts. Wouldn't it be a wonderful thing for all of our activities to be conditioned by the pattern of faith instead of distorted patterns of fear and worry and disease?

It has been written, "As we think in our heart, so we are." Science has explained the reason why, and modern religion tells us what to do about it. There is before us now the use of a practical faith which endows us with a creative power that each of us can use to heal ourselves of the scourge of anxiety. When we stop and consciously realize that everything life is is right where we are, we can come to a place of certainty in our own minds where we no longer feel that we are lacking. There is only one life, which is God, the power greater than we are, and each of us is an expression of this one life. Nothing is more certain in the universe than the infinite presence of good. When we are conscious of the infinite presence of good, this certainty is reflected in all that we do. It is reflected in our attitudes toward work, toward other people, and toward ourselves.

Life is sufficient unto itself. It lacks nothing. It needs nothing. It is all there is, everywhere present. If, through our faith and our belief, we capture this vision and hold it as a pattern before the mirror of our own mind, it will automatically follow that we will become confident and courageous, instead of timid and afraid.

But before we can do this, we must come sincerely and simply to believe that there is a power greater than we are and that we can use it. We must come to believe that This Thing Called Life desires only that which is good for us. This is all it has ever planned. All of these other things that have so unhappily been lodged in our minds were put there by fear, ignorance, and doubt. This fear and uncertainty which has so burdened us has been based on the lack of a realization that everyone has a silent partner who accompanies them through life. They have been trying to go entirely on their own, so to speak.

Right here is where faith must enter, because it makes no difference how much we know about the laws of Mind. It isn't enough just to know that our minds are mirrors reflecting our inward unconscious thoughts into our everyday lives. What we need to add to this is something that spiritual conviction alone can give us.

What is it that we are reflecting? Here is something

that is good to know. Before we ever reflected a neurotic pattern of any kind, we reflected a divine pattern, whole and perfect, which is still with us and which will always be with us. It is in no way subject to the limitation of time or the sequence of events. It is the eternal now, the everlasting here, and the God who has never deserted its creation.

Someone may say, "You're trying to lead us back to religion." I am not trying to lead anybody anywhere. I am merely pointing out some facts that are now proven to be so. We are rooted in pure Spirit and in perfect life, and we will be freed from fear and doubt and worry only when we find a faith and a confidence and a conviction greater than our former limitation. For every fear, we must find a faith, and we must substitute certainty for uncertainty.

Just put this to work and see what happens. Say to yourself, "There is something within me that is never afraid, no matter what the appearances may be. There is something within me that is never anxious, because it knows that everything is all right in spite of my feeble and futile worries." Say to yourself, and mean it, "I am endowed with courage and confidence. I face life with the seed of victory in my attitudes and my expectations."

Know that as you go forward from this point, life holds only the best for you, and even as you begin to think and move in such a direction, you will discover blessings in all that you do greater than you might have dared to dream while you stood quaking before the ghosts of your former fears. Faith is the only complete answer to our worries—faith in something greater than we are.

. . .

Meditation

I am now established in the presence of infinite good. The life of God is my life right now. The mind of God is my mind right now.

I open my heart to the influx of Spirit and know that the love that floods my being heals my body and dispels every shadow of doubt and fear and anxiety.

The truth of my spiritual being sets me free from the bondage of ignorance. Divine intelligence directs my thoughts and my path, so that I may move into life's activities with a calm poise and assurance that never wavers.

I dwell in the house of the Lord forever and rejoice in the divine companionship of the infinite presence that sustains me in all I do. All that the Creator has is mine. This I accept. This I express.

How to

GROW BETTER DAY BY DAY

. . .

When Emil Coue came to this country a number of years ago, he brought with him a piece of string with twenty knots in it and an idea, of which the string was a symbol. His idea was that if you run your fingers over the twenty knots, repeating rapidly, "Every day and in every way, I am becoming better and better," you will finally arrive at an affirmative realization of life. His piece of string was a method for changing the thought patterns that are more or less set within our minds.

He had already experimented in France with several thousand patients and had gotten good results. The reason he repeated the affirmation twenty times was that he believed the suggestion must become auto-suggestion before it can become self-realization, and self-realization is necessary to a change in our consciousness. This means that a new idea must be deeply rooted before it can be effective. It must become a conviction rather than a surface suggestion. It must actually be an inward self-realization, which he called *auto-suggestion*.

In working this out, he discovered that when the will and the imagination are in conflict, it is the imagination, and not the will, that wins. This is because imagination is a thing of feeling, while the will is a thing of the intellect. Not that there is anything wrong with the will, because in a certain sense one would use will to stimulate imagination. But it is the imagination that is the real creative factor within us.

It was Coue's concept that most of our troubles, whether they be physical or of any other nature, are a result of negative thought patterns so deeply buried in the mind that they work almost unconsciously.

Now let us look back nearly two thousand years and listen to the words of wisdom of the one whose spiritual genius stands out so boldly across the pages of human history. If there is anyone who ever lived who knew the answers to the problems of humanity, it was Jesus. Jesus most certainly said that the realm of God is within us, that every individual life is rooted in the living Spirit, and that everyone has a direct, immediate, and personal relationship to this living Spirit.

The self-realization, then, that Coue sought to arrive at through breaking down negative thought patterns was fundamentally right. The negative thought patterns we have to break down are those mental states that deny our divine heritage, that would make us believe that we are separated, isolated, and alone, struggling against uneven odds and with only dismal hope for success.

Jesus, who understood life better than anyone else, said, "It is done unto you as you believe." But he added, "Who, by taking thought, can add one cubit to one's stature?" At first this seems a contradiction, until we understand its meaning.

When we discover an energy in nature and how to use it, we realize that it is not because of our willpower of taking thought that it operates, because our taking thought and our will were merely the mental instruments we used to discover something that is self-operating.

We take thought and make a conscious decision when we wire a building for electric lights, and yet our thought does not create the energy that lights the building. It merely channels it. It decides how we are going to use it. We are always using silent forces in nature that seem to be flowing through everything and everyone. For instance, we set up a generator by a waterfall and take out energy. The generator is a mechanical thing; our use of the power that flows through this mechanical instrument is our will and our choice.

There is another kind of a waterfall and another kind of a mechanical instrument through which it flows. This other kind of energy is a spiritual power flowing through our thought. Jesus had set up his generator in such a relationship to This Thing Called Life and the law of good that he was able at all times and under every circumstance to draw on a spiritual energy that flowed through him into action. He used this energy to heal the sick, to raise the dead, to give sight to the blind, and in a hundred other ways.

Jesus did not say, "I am the only one who knows about the eternal waterfall or the law of good." He did not say, "I am the only one who has a generator." He did not say, "I am the only one whom God has chosen to use this power." This is exactly what Jesus never did say, because he was not only the most inspired, he was also the most intelligent person who ever lived.

What Jesus did say was, "What I have done, you can do also." He said, "Watch what I am doing and learn how to do it for yourself." But in some peculiar way, we have tried to interpret the words of Jesus as though they didn't mean exactly what they said. As a matter of fact, Jesus meant what he said and said what he meant, nothing more and nothing less. This is the great mistake we have made. This is the error we have fallen into.

The reason for this is simple enough. It seems too good to be true. It doesn't seem possible that we could repeat a few simple thoughts over and over and have them finally break down our doubts and fears until we emerge into a place of calm and certainty. And it doesn't seem possible that prayer could be answered when we pray without ceasing, which means when our whole thought becomes affirmative.

Why doesn't it seem possible? Because we have missed the fundamental idea that there is a spiritual self, that God really is right where we are, that just as we use the laws of nature for definite purposes in our mechanical endeavors, so we may also use spiritual and mental laws for definite purposes. Since we look around and see so much that contradicts this, we fail to arrive at that deep, imaginative feeling of conviction that every artist must arrive at before they can paint a great picture.

The miracles of Jesus were as natural to him as are the signs following any inventive genius. The presence of God in him and around him and through him and everyone was as real to Jesus as the feeling of beauty is to a great artist. The divine energy and the law of good that Jesus used were as natural and real to him as the laws of physics are to a physicist. Jesus was not the great exception; he was the great example. He was the way-shower.

It doesn't matter how exalted the person is who shows us the way; we have to walk in it. If we are traveling and ask for directions, how to get from one place to another, someone by the roadside or at the gas station may tell us what road to take because they have been there. But if we say, "Well, that isn't the road I want to travel, and I don't like it" or "I don't believe there is such a road," then of course we will never arrive at that destination. It really is all very simple.

Suppose we get a little piece of string and tie twenty knots in it, only instead of a string, let's imagine that we have an idea that we are willing to remind ourselves of every hour in the day, a sort of a rosary of faith. And suppose we actually use it. At first, it might seem a little unreal to us, a little vague and indefinite. The intellect cannot quite see the way ahead. The world is so big and problems are so multiplied. But the heart already knows. Life has placed an intuition, a feeling, within us. God has given us a guide. As Job said, "There is a spirit in humankind, and the inspiration of the Almighty gives understanding."

Let's follow this feeling out and see if it will not lead us to a place of faith and conviction. If we are persistent in it, it will certainly lead us to a place of demonstration, to a place where we actually know because we have really experienced the use of a power greater than we are.

There are two courses we can take. We can deny the whole thing and say it is too good to be true or an idle dream. Or we can conclude that the whole scheme of things must make sense and there must be a way, a truth, and a life. We can actually believe that Jesus meant what he said when he told us that he came to bear witness to the truth that God is right where we are, that the law of good is available.

This is the path we wish to follow. At first, it may seem dim and the sign posts blurred. But gradually, like the pilgrim of old, as we make the ascent from the canyons of unbelief to the mountain tops of realization, we will find that, with each step in our progress, our burdens roll away and our fears depart like thieves in the night.

Someone once said to me, "How do you know that what you believe is not all an illusion? Perhaps it is just wishful thinking, a flight of fancy in your own imagination." This person asked, "How do you know?"

I replied, "Suppose you take someone who seems alone and friendless, so lonely they don't know what to do with themselves. And you convince this person to count a rosary of faith with definite thought and feeling every day over a period of time, and after awhile this person comes to you and says, 'My whole life has changed. Everywhere I go, I meet with love and friendship.' Do you think you could convince that person that they have been lost in a fantastic dream or merely submerged in a wishful thinking? Of course not!"

I said to my friend, "In this, as in everything else, the proof of the pudding is in the eating. If, through spiritual power, through prayer or faith or meditation or whatever one chooses to call it, good can be brought into a life, which harms no one but which increases livingness, that person will become thoroughly convinced that there is a power greater than they are, a power of good that they can use."

This is the position you and I find ourselves in today. Day by day, we are either getting better and better, or day by day we are following the same monotonous path of uncertainty, because we all have knots in our string of life that we would like to re-tie.

This will call for a little self-training, but it is worthwhile, and surely it is up to us to make the experiment, no doubt the greatest experiment we can or will ever make—the adventure of self-discovery, of self-realization, the adventure of finding the real self hidden beneath all our doubts and fears and uncertainties, the self we all would like to be.

. . .

Meditation

Prayer is spiritual communion, and the ideas used in meditation are for the purpose of breaking down the negative thought patterns that deny the good we so greatly need and so earnestly seek. Prayer, spiritual communion, and meditation, to be effective, should be direct, personal, and immediate, so that the words used may become self-realization.

.

Believing that the Spirit of God is at the center of my own being and at the center of all others, I now invite this divine presence to illumine my thought, to guide me in everything I do.

In this quiet moment of self-realization, I feel that I am meeting this divine presence face to face.

I feel that all the vitality there is, all the energy there is, and all the enthusiasm for life that there is is flowing through me, circulating through every atom of my physical being, animating every organ, every action, and every function of my physical body with perfect life.

I feel the inflow and the circulation of this Spirit through me, and in joy and gladness I recognize the presence of love and life.

Surely this is the realm of God.

This is the day that God has made, and I am glad in it.

How to
TALK TO GOD

. . .

Prayer, the desire to reach out to something greater than we are, has been common to every age. Instinctively, we feel that there is a higher power, a greater intelligence that responds to us. Our minds reach out with feeling and faith to a "something" that will respond to us, a "something" that is always available.

The human mind needs and must have a direct approach to Spirit. It is natural for us to reach out from our ignorance to this Spirit's enlightenment, from our weakness to its strength, from our darkness to its light. We feel and know that this Spirit is right where we are.

Somewhere along the line, we will have to surrender our weakness to its strength, our fear to its faith, our lack to its abundance.

We need not ask how we should reach out to God. All we need do is reach. When we each reach in our own way, we will be fulfilling the nature of our own being. No good can come from waiting until someone tells us just how, because their "just how" could never be our "just how." Everyone will have to discover their own "just how," and it will be right. It seems as though it would have to be direct and simple, personal and immediate, reaching out from a feeling of need, with an equal feeling that the need will be met—reaching out with faith.

Jesus said that the very hairs of our head are numbered, that not a sparrow falls to the ground without God knowing it. Wouldn't it be wonderful to feel that we are cradled in such a love and wisdom and to know that divine power is immediately available to all of us?

Since we need it so much and we feel we can no longer live without it, we are going to act as though it were right here, always responding to us, loving us in spite of our mistakes. We will lay at the feet of such love all our weakness and uncertainty, all our past mistakes, and say, "I am no longer afraid of them. I know they are going to be lost in something greater."

Let's not be afraid to commune with this "something" that is greater than we are individually or in groups. It is wonderful for people to get together and pool their faith, each upholding the conviction of the other. It is like singing in the chorus. It is like an anthem of life and hope.

One person's faith strengthens another's. Sometimes it seems as though we each bring a feeble lamp into a great, dark hall and, lifting up our lamp, find its rays joined with those of others until all darkness disappears and a great light fills the room.

As the disciples watched Jesus in his ministry, they saw light come into the eyes of those without vision. They saw a new energy flowing through the limbs of those who were paralyzed. They saw the lame walk, the mute speak, and the deaf hear.

They asked Jesus to teach them how to pray, and Jesus said, "When you tell God what you want, you should believe that God is going to give it to you." He was definite about this, because he said that when you ask God for something, you should believe not only that God is going to give it to you, but that God already has given it to you.

The very simplicity of this thought confounds us. Can even God give us something we don't take? The sun is shining, but we must step out of the shadow if we are to receive its rays. It all seems too good to be true, and yet Jesus announced with the utmost simplicity that God is right where we are and responds to us, that God is greater than we are, and can and wants to help us, and that God will do it when we believe God will do it.

. . .

Meditation

God's ever-present life is flowing through me and around me now. I know that God, the divine and perfect Spirit, is right where I am. I know that there is a loving presence around me. I know that I live, move, and have my being in the life of Spirit. It is my desire that only that which is good, peaceful, loving, and life-giving will flow through me to others.

Therefore, I bless everything I do, everyone I meet, every situation in which I find myself, and I know that God blesses everything I do and everyone I meet and every situation I find myself in. I believe that all my needs are met by divine love and that I am guided by a divine intelligence that cannot fail.

My whole faith is lifted up to a power greater than I am. I believe that this power governs, guides, sustains, and directs me. I believe it flows through me to bless others. I believe in God, the living Spirit Almighty, and I believe in God here and now, today.

PLANT YOUR MENTAL GARDEN

. . .

In springtime, many people begin setting out their gardens. People visit nurseries, purchase seeds, and decide what they wish to plant. Spring is a joyful season of the year, filled with hope and expectancy, vibrant with the miracle of life. Every clod of earth seems to stir with new animation, as though something were coming alive inside it. Every little seed is bursting with joy. The birds are building their nests and all nature is fashioning new apparel for itself.

What is our part in this great scheme of things, in this power greater than we are that gives us seed time and harvest? Let's look at the garden of the mind and what can happen when it is impregnated with the creative power of This Thing Called Life.

Spring is a time for new beginnings, an opportunity for a fresh approach to life. It is the time when we use the creative law of life for the purpose of producing our selected harvest. But we are interested in another kind of seed and another kind of gardening—the garden of the mind, the soil of faith, and the seed of hope. Today we are going to plant some seeds. Later we will cultivate them, and then we will deal with the harvest.

In the spring, we go into our gardens filled with hope. We lay out our plots of ground and decide just what we wish nature to produce for us during the summer. We wait with enthusiastic interest on a miraculous and wonder-working law for the first evidence that our seed of hope has been accepted and that we may confidently look forward to a harvest.

Before we begin planting our gardens, let's consider one of the parables of Jesus, the parable of the sower, in which a certain farmer went out to sow seeds. Some of the seed fell on barren soil and some on good, while some fell on rocks and some was carried away by the wind. Jesus tells us that the seed that fell into good soil increased a hundredfold.

Jesus, wisest of the wise, brought us these simple nature lessons to show that just as there is a law of creation working in the most common garden plot, so there is another and a similar law of This Thing Called Life working in the garden of our minds. When his disciples asked him to interpret the meaning of this parable, he said that the seed is the word, by which he meant our thoughts and feelings, our mental attitudes toward life. Jesus told us that these words, these seed-thoughts that we sow in the garden of the mind, should be thoughts of faith, of love, of hope, and over and over again he tells us that they must be thoughts of acceptance.

We are so accustomed to planting something in the earth and having it grow that we accept this miracle of nature as an ordinary event. We lay out our rows and plant our seeds with a happy and an enthusiastic expectancy. We are as childlike about this as a little child asking its parent for supper.

Good gardeners take joy in what they are doing and are happy over the prospect. Yet, the best gardeners must rely completely on the laws of nature because they know that no seed can take root until it is planted and that there can be no harvest until the seed is first hid away in the creative law of nature.

This is just as much an act faith as though you were praying for something. But the faith you have in planting your garden is complete. It is relaxed. You do not question whether or not life will give you a harvest. Experience has taught you that it will. Don't you think this same truth holds good in the law of Mind and Spirit?

Jesus said that we should watch and pray when we prepare the soil of the mind in order that the warmth of God's sunshine and the refreshment of God's gentle rain may penetrate the soil of our mind and turn it into a rich soil of love. In mental gardening, thought is the seed that, through the law of love, can heal, enrich, and expand your experience. "As you think in your heart, so you are." As we continually think deep in our inward conviction, so will we become.

We are all sowers in the garden of the mind, and here is something that perhaps we hadn't thought of. This garden of the mind is freely given to us by This Thing Called Life, by a power greater than we are. We received a deed for it when we were born, and the title is good because life itself gave it to us.

In a certain sense, we are not much different from the most primitive people because the last gardeners on earth will have to do what the first ones did. They will have to plant their seed and care for it while it grows if they hope to reap a harvest. The first gardeners did not make the seed fertile, nor did they put into the soil that which makes the seed grow. This Thing Called Life produces both the seed and the harvest.

Though we grind the seed to powder, we will never disclose the principle of life within it that makes it grow. We can hold the seed in our hand while we doubt and argue and while others deny its potency, and we will neither have changed nor destroyed the thing within it that is alive. But whoever we are and wherever we are, we can plant that seed in the soil and, in perfect faith, wait to see it come into form. This is the eternal miracle of our being, forever old, forever new.

In preparing your mental garden for the harvest of faith, you must break down all doubt and unbelief. You must uproot the weeds of fear. You must rake the garden free from obstructions so that your thoughts may flow freely through it. Above all else, you must cultivate a childlike faith and expectancy.

The laws of Mind, like the laws of the earth, have always been with us, and wise spiritual gardeners have always used them. It would be wonderful if, by some magic trick, we could arrive at as complete a faith in the law of good as we have in other laws of nature. This is why Jesus tells us that we must become as little children, "for of such is the realm of God."

Imagine if you had always had a secret ambition to own a ranch. How wonderful you would feel if someone were to tell you that before you were born your ancestors had deeded one to you. It would be hard for you to believe. You might say, "I didn't even know my ancestors. Moreover, it hard to believe that they could have left me such a property as you describe." But this is exactly like what Jesus tells us is true.

It has taken two thousand years for us to come to a place where we actually believe that Jesus knew what he was talking about, that he really said what he meant and actually meant what he said. Even the parable of Eden was written to show this, because surely the Garden of Eden is the garden of life that humankind was given so that we might till it and produce from the abundance of nature the fruit of the vine and the orchard, the milk and honey of the Promised Land.

Isn't it strange that we have possessed this land in truth and in reality without possessing it in our experience? We have been walking across the vast acreage of life's garden looking for fertile plains and valleys. We have been seeking mountain canyons through which course the refreshing rivers of life flow, forever renewed by the eternal snows from heaven, and we haven't found them. Yet Jesus said, "Behold, the realm is at hand." He said to look more closely, think more deeply, believe more completely, accept more unconditionally. He told us that faith in God's bounty is the seed of wealth brought forth into form through our faith in the invisible.

Let us ask ourselves this simple question: When we go into our garden in the spring of the year and think about planting it, and decide what we want to be in this row and that row and where we wish to put the berry bushes and the strawberry vines, or plant the onions and cabbages and maybe a shade tree, do we actually see these things objectively? There is no vine there yet. There is no shade tree. There are no strawberry plants. There is nothing but the bare and apparently barren soil. All we have is a little seed we hold in our hand, the seed of hope and faith that gives promise of its own fulfillment through the law of good.

Jesus said, "Blessed are they that have not seen and yet have believed." The wonderful thing about all the parables of Jesus is that they are simple illustrations of how it is that the invisible—that which you do not see—through God's law of creation can produce that which you long for, that which your highest hope has placed as the goal of your greatest attainment. Jesus summed it all up in two words: *faith* and *belief.* We need not doubt the invisible. We need not doubt its nature or its law.

We wish now to plant seeds in the springtime of our hope, which through careful cultivation will produce the fruit of love and accomplishment, and we wish that this springtime and summer and fall—the planting, the cultivation, and the harvest—will be one joyful season of expectancy.

And here is a wonderful thing. *We are permitted to select the seeds.* We, of our own volition, are allowed to plant them in the garden of life, but the only power that can give them fruit is This Thing Called Life.

What, then, will we plant? First of all, let's be sure that we plant only that which we wish to reap, because "as we sow, so shall we also reap." Let's be certain that our seeds are planted in love, because God is love and love is God. Love alone makes the world a better place in which to live. Love alone, felt and expressed, makes our lives worthwhile. Without love, all living is a poor business, empty and unhappy. Love must be the first impulsion of our planting.

Next, we must use the seed of faith, because it is only through faith that we dare let the seed slip from our hand into the creative soil which alone can produce a plant. We mustn't be afraid to bury that love and faith deep in the soil of hope, because hope lightens the soil.

We must plant with understanding. That is, we must understand that our simple, sincere thoughts are actually seeds that, in the garden of life, can produce a variety of experiences. If you were to say to a gardener of the soil, "I have never planted a seed, never made a garden. How can I work this miracle?" The gardener might say to you, "Here are a number of seeds. They are small, hard, and drab in color, entirely unprepossessing in appearance, but in each rests the miracle of life. This one will become a lilac; this a sweet pea; this a petunia; this a nasturtium."

In like manner, we must decide what mental seed we most want to plant and under what general heading it comes—health, success, love, or self-expression. Do you want better general health? Do you feel that you need a greater measure of supply? Would your happiness be increased if you had more friends? If so, be sure that you plant the seeds that are like your desire.

As you cultivate the soil of your mind, be certain that each day your thoughts are a little more pliable, a little less resistant, a little more peaceful and poised, a little more expectant of the good.

So plant your seeds. Care for them lovingly, devotedly, and do not be concerned with anything except the thoughts you think and not with the time or the process of their growth and flowering. That is the work of creative mind soil. Your job is simply to "be still and know" that you are drawing on the Infinite, that all the faith and hope you plant in the garden of your mind will someday spring forth into glorious abundance.

. . .

Meditation

Meditation does two things for us. One, we might call passive, and the other, active. By passive, we mean that meditation helps us to recognize the divine presence and feel it deep within our own being, and then helps us to realize that the Spirit within us is at one with the Spirit of God. The active part of meditation is where we use the law of good for definite purposes, because we are all surrounded by a creative Mind that responds to our belief in it.

Let us see if we cannot realize that our faith acts as a seed planted in the creative soil. We do the planting, but God gives us the harvest.

.

Believing that my word is the seed of good, and that the divine giver of all life wills me to have a harvest, I plant this seed in the warm, rich soil of divine love and bury it in my faith. I know that from this seed, which is my word, and from that power of good greater than I am, which is the law of God, I will receive a harvest.

This is the springtime of my hope, and I desire that love, peace, and confidence will envelop me and everyone I meet as I sit in the garden of God, my Garden of Eden. I desire that joy and happiness will go forth from me to make glad the life of every other person. As I wait on the Spirit, I am planting seeds of happiness, of friendship, of love, of goodwill for myself, for everyone I know, and for the whole world.

Not alone in my garden do I wish these seeds to grow, but I pray that I may broadcast them wherever I walk. Uniting with all others in faith, I rest in the supreme assurance that the life that the whole world seeks will find fruitage in the garden of love that I am planting today.

CULTIVATE YOUR MENTAL GARDEN

. . .

After we have planted a garden, we must cultivate it. We must keep it free from weeds. In the garden of the mind, this means that, having planted the right thoughts, we must carefully nurture them and see that they do not become uprooted by doubt and fear. Now you are going to learn how to cultivate your mental garden so it will produce health, happiness, and success.

In the previous chapter, we talked about planting seeds of hope in the fertile soil of your faith in This Thing Called Life. Initially, there seems to be a difference between mental gardening and earthly gardening, but we see that the law of planting is the same in both instances because the soil of the mind must be prepared even as we prepare the earth to receive the seeds we wish to plant.

It seems wonderful to think of the garden of the mind just as we do another kind of a garden, and to realize that a power greater than we are actually produces the harvest. It is life that gives us this garden; it is the law of God that causes it to grow. But as the Old Testament tells us in the story of the Garden of Eden, humankind was given the garden to tend and water, and this garden means our plot in the creative Mind of the universe. Since we have planted seeds in this garden, we now wish to be certain we are cultivating them rightly so that they may receive the warmth of God's sunshine and the refreshing rains of the outpouring of God's love.

Our garden is a garden of thoughts and ideas, of hope and of faith from which will grow, if we carefully tend it, the fruit of our heart's desire. Don't you think it is interesting to realize that the simplest child who pokes a tiny seed into the ground with a little finger will receive a harvest equal to that of a Luther Burbank, who spent his whole life in horticulture? Perhaps this is why Jesus said, "I thank you that you have hid these things from the wise and the prudent and have revealed them to babes."

Luther Burbank produced plants new to nature because he was in partnership with This Thing Called Life. I never had the privilege of meeting Luther Burbank, but his wife once told me that he actually talked to his plants and told them what he wanted them to do. Life has given us all the power to do something new, and if you cultivate your garden carefully, you too may find, when the harvest comes, that something new and wonderful has been created for you.

Your mind is really the place where you use the mind of This Thing Called Life. The fruits that appear in your garden and the plants you are to harvest are the gifts of a power greater than you are. We call this *the gift*, or *life*.

As we plant the seeds, God gives us the harvest. We have planted seeds of hope. Let's be certain that we cultivate them with loving attention and with the enthusiastic expectancy that every gardener has. Let's remember that we are dealing with the miracle of life, and let's see if we can keep the childlike wonder that is so necessary to our everyday happiness.

One always feels enthusiastic when meeting people who have enthusiasm. When you talk with those who have faith, your own faith is increased. The very contact of a lovable personality warms the heart, cheers the mind and restores confidence in life.

You must certainly keep the wonder of life alive in your imagination and keep your mind warm with the feeling of growing things—new things that are going to come into your experience—because you are cultivating the garden of God.

What about the weeds that are almost certain to appear? In your physical garden, you go out resolutely and pull them up. You expose their roots to the heat of the sun, and soon they wither away. It is the same in the garden of your mind. Doubts will appear and uncertainty may break through, but now, like a good gardener, you are going to uproot them.

Perhaps you are saying to yourself, "How am I going to do this?" Here is the secret. It is so very simple that it seems almost unbelievable. However, it is true. *Thoughts are things.* Just as a thought of fear will produce a wrong result, so the opposite thought, which is faith, will produce an opposite result.

If fear appears in your garden, dig it up with the hoe of faith, and say to it, "You have no business here at all. I have nothing to be afraid of. My garden is the garden of God, and God has never put anything here to be afraid of."

If you go out in your garden some morning and find that a weed of uncertainty has made its appearance in the row where you have planted the seeds of confidence, just say to yourself, "Why should I be uncertain? I am dealing with the only power there is. God isn't uncertain, and I don't have to be. I have put my whole confidence in a power greater than I am, and I know that there is nothing that can break its law, nothing that can retard its harvest."

Perhaps when you go out into your garden in the cool of the evening and look up and down the rows to see how beautifully they are growing, you may discover something that looks strange. You see, this garden is yourself, and sometimes you may find something growing there that tells you that you don't like people and they don't like you, that you just don't fit into the whole scheme of life. This is an unnatural growth, and, like other weeds, it must be rooted out.

So you will say to yourself, "There is only one Mind, one Spirit, one God, and nothing can grow in my garden that denies the union of all life. Of course I like people, and of course they like me. Why shouldn't they? As a matter of fact, I have a great love for everyone in my heart, a great longing to enter into the joy and, wherever necessary, the pain and the sorrow of others." You can say to yourself, "Let us walk together in God's garden, dearest heart, not apart, because those who know the joys and sorrows other lives have known never walk alone."

By using simple thoughts like these, but ones that grow out of deep and sincere conviction, you will uproot the thoughts that deny you the privilege of loving and of being loved. So you are cultivating your garden day by day, and it is growing wonderfully. Your expectancy is high and you are looking forward to the harvest with keenest anticipation.

Much to your surprise, some beautiful morning when you go out in the sunshine to cultivate your garden, you may find that the crabgrass of failure and discontent has been choking your plants. Of course you didn't mean it this way and you didn't intend it this way, but this is human experience. This is what you and I and everyone else occasionally meet.

There is only one thing you can do. Pull it up! And do it directly, not as though you were antagonistic toward this weed or as though it had any power over you, because that isn't the way you would feel if you were weeding your garden. You would simply say, "That doesn't belong here, so up it comes and out it goes."

Your garden is beginning to look pretty good by now. Yet, as you look down the rows in which you have planted your seeds, there is another thing that may cause you to wonder a little. Some of the plants seem to come up faster than others. Radishes will make their appearance in a few days in your physical garden if your soil is right, and so will many other plants. But it takes a longer for an acorn to sprout and send forth its sturdy shoots that someday will become a giant shade tree.

Perhaps you have buried some thoughts and aspirations in the garden of your mind that don't seem to be showing any signs of life. Perhaps in the secret desire of your heart, you have told God about a lot of things you would like to have happen, things that are to influence your life and remain with you forever. These are the sturdy plants, deep-rooted, high-climbing, broad-spreading.

Yes, some of the seeds you plant may not appear for some time, but you still must pour the water of your faith over them. Above everything else, be sure that you don't pull them up to see if they are sprouting. Just leave them alone, quietly in the womb of nature. To "be still and know" at a time like this will be a wonderful thought for you. The law of the universe is at work in your behalf, and with a happy heart you may go about your daily living, knowing that the Lord of all creation has heard your request.

There are a few other things that we must carefully and tenderly care for. We live in a world where there is too much unbelief, too much skepticism, too much confusion. You see it everywhere, and too often you hear it in ordinary conversations. When you are at home alone and thinking things over quietly, you build up a great confidence in life. Then when you go out into the world, which everyone must and should wish to do, you see so much that contradicts those wonderful thoughts that have come to you when you were alone.

The suggestion of your environment can do a lot in planting the wrong kinds of seeds in your garden, but you can do a lot more than this because you can pull them all up. You can refuse to see them. You can refuse to listen to them. Something within you can become adamant to them until finally they disappear altogether.

Of course, you have to live with the world, and you wouldn't wish it to be otherwise. Sometimes out of pretty tough experience you will learn how to cultivate the garden of your mind. Sometimes the greatest of all miracles is the growth of the seeds that are planted in barren soil. How highly we prize those plants growing from the rocks on the sides of the mountains or the trees that grow in a city street!

God's garden is everywhere, and your faith will be always rewarded with a sign. A tiny shoot thrusts its head out and upward toward the sunshine. So your thoughts of faith will break down every negative environment, and as you find courage to live perhaps in the face of doubt and unbelief, you will find that even what appeared to be barren spots have a deep, rich earth beneath them.

God's garden is everywhere, and wherever you go you will have the tools to cultivate this garden. They were placed in your hand by a power and an intelligence greater than yours.

Every experiment in scientific advance is an experiment that people of great faith in the laws of nature are carrying out, and gradually new forms are appearing, new ways of doing things, because someone had the courage to wait and work and sing. Above everything else, I would like that you sing and perhaps dance a little up and down the rows you have planted in your garden.

There is always a song somewhere for those who have trained their ears to hear. There is always a song somewhere. Sing it!

. . .

Meditation

Today you cultivate your garden. You pull up the weeds of uncertainty and carefully nurture your thoughts of faith and confidence in This Thing Called Life, in the power greater than you are, in God the living Spirit. Do not be weary in well doing, because in due season you will reap if you faint not. As you carry this simple thought back into your mind, you are lifting up your whole thought to the sunshine and rain from heaven, and you are knowing that a power greater than you are is seeing to it that the seeds of your expectancy are sprouting in the garden of your desire.

.

I have planted my garden, and I know that the Lord of the harvest will give the increase. As I go about the everyday activities of living, I confidently expect to meet with happiness and with success. I believe that deep within me is the well-spring of eternal life. I believe that around me is the joy of living. I believe that I am sustained by a divine power and guided by an infinite wisdom.

No thought of fear can assail me, no doubt can enter my consciousness, no uncertainty can grow in my garden, because I have planted it in the mind of God. I have planted it with hope, with conviction, and in certainty. I am waiting the harvest with a song of joy in my heart.

I have not planted this garden for myself alone, but that I may share it with others. I will have plenty to spare, an abundance of love, an excess of goodwill. I have planted tenderness and compassion here so that others may come and eat of the fruits of the garden of life with me. There will be no strangers in my garden, because God's sun and rain come alike to the garden of every soul. I enter into communion with others as I walk in the garden of life and sit under the shade tree of peace and love.

How to
HARVEST YOUR MENTAL GARDEN

. . .

The more I think about the garden of the mind, the more interested I become in the subject. It seems so filled with limitless possibilities for good. I can tell you that I have made several changes in my own planting. I found some plants there that it seemed wise to uproot and to plant something more worthwhile in their place, and maybe you have had the same experience.

None of us is perfect, and yet we all have a yearning for something better. I believe with Emerson that we should keep our vision high and hitch our wagon to a star. We should keep our vision high and do everything in our power to attain the goal of our heart's desire.

Now we are going to see what our harvest looks like

so far, what increase we may expect from our planting and cultivation. I know that we are going to reap a good crop, not only of thoughts and ideas, but of actual experiences.

We have seen how our physical gardens are planted in the soil of the warm, rich earth that gives back an increase, and we have likened this to the soil of the mind in which are planted the seeds of thoughts and ideas, the seed of the earth and the seed of a thought, the harvesting of the abundance of nature and the harvesting of our thoughts and feelings. We have learned that the soil of the mind, like the earth, must first be prepared if we wish This Thing Called Life—the power greater than we are—to give us the desired harvest.

We have tried to plant in love and to cultivate our gardens with expectant enthusiasm. We have tried to be happy gardeners and to plant our seeds in faith. Love, happiness, and faith are the three most fundamental things in life. We have discussed how it is that seeds of thought planted in the soil of the mind will produce a harvest exactly like the seed, because we are dealing with a law in nature. We have also considered another important thought. When we plant seeds, we must leave them alone. We must not pull them up or expose their roots to the sun lest they wither and die.

We have come to realize that there is no difference between sowing ideas in the mind and sowing seed in the soil, because the same law works in both instances. We are surrounded by an infinite Mind that receives the impress of our thought and acts on it creatively.

This is the simple key to the whole situation. This is why Jesus said, "It is done unto you as you believe." We have overlooked this simple thought—"It is done unto you"—which means that there is a power greater than we are in which we live, one that, like a mirror, reflects back to us those things we have pictured in our inward thought.

I like to think about this garden of the mind, this deep, rich spiritual soil that life has given us to cultivate. I like to realize that nothing can rob us of this garden, because we have the privilege and the joy of cultivating it and watching it grow as faith takes form and gives back to us the harvest of our fondest hope.

We have learned how necessary it is to guard against fear, how we must cultivate the assurance of faith and hope. Now we come to the harvest, and in this harvest we should expect that every seed will have multiplied, providing seeds for another planting and another harvest, because this is one of the rewards of gardening: the bountiful increase of nature.

Plant one little melon seed and it will give you a vine and a fruit that multiplies your endeavor a hundred times. You will have seed enough to set out a much larger patch in a new season and an abundance left over to give your neighbors. How wonderful is this gift of life, and how extravagant the increase of good! The great teacher Jesus said, "Give, and it shall be given unto you; good measure, pressed down and shaken together, and running over." The final act of the harvest is one of gratefulness and thanksgiving, thankfulness to the great principle of life for the completed cycle and the fulfillment of our desires.

I would like to tell you how this worked in the life of a music teacher I once knew. This teacher gave piano lessons, but wasn't able to get many pupils. In analyzing the creative soil of her mind, I discovered that practically all she had planted there were thoughts of doubt and failure. Way down inside her, she really didn't expect pupils. I asked her why. Her main reasons seemed to be that she had no influential friends and there were so many others in the same profession. There was too much competition and she never seemed to meet the right people.

So we had to pull up a lot of weeds and get rid of some crabgrass, and then plant some seeds of hope and expectancy. Since she was rather depressed, we had to uproot anxiety and plant faith and confidence. In actual practice, I told her to expect pupils, to daily affirm that whoever could be benefited by her services would be brought to her by the law of good. I explained to her that there is only one Mind, God's Mind, that this Mind is present everywhere and that it would be easy enough for it to bring her more pupils than she could possibly have time to teach.

It took a little time for the replanting and the careful cultivation of the soil of her mind, but almost from the start there were signs following her belief, just as Jesus told us there always would be when he said, "These signs shall follow them that believe." These signs began to follow the change of her belief, and as her whole inner thought changed—those deep-laid thought patterns, which in the long run really decide what is going to happen to us—things began to happen.

After a few months of careful cultivation, the garden of her mind began to yield a harvest, in about the same time it takes to plant a garden in the soil and receive a harvest. It really was a natural process. When the harvest time came, she told me that it seemed as though everywhere she went people would ask her what was her profession, and when she told them that she taught piano, they would say, "I would like to take some lessons" or "I have a friend who would like to" or "I have a child who ought to."

What really happened was that she had removed the weeds. She had uprooted the doubts and fears. She had acquired faith and confidence, and all by the process of making a few simple affirmations every day. This was really "praying without ceasing" until it became a habit.

A constructive habit is just as easily acquired as a destructive one—in fact, I believe more easily acquired—because there is a vitality in affirmation that is lacking in the denials of life. Affirmation acts like light overcoming darkness. Darkness is a negation; light is a positive affirmation, and where there is light, there is no darkness.

As you look out over the fields you have planted and the soil you have cultivated so patiently, you have a right to expect a harvest. Nature will never let you down. This Thing Called Life is for you and not against you, and the power greater than you are is ready, willing, and waiting to supply your every need. All that the garden of life asks is that you believe in it, that you have faith in it.

If you have planted seeds of friendship, you should expect to be rewarded, and I don't mean in any uncertain sense, because if you have really planted seeds of friendship and cultivated your garden in a friendly manner, you have a right to harvest love and friendship. I want you to be certain that this doesn't remain merely a good symbol or a happy thought in your mind, or a sort of an idle dream. When you plant, you are bound to reap, and the harvest you reap will be like the seeds you have planted.

If it doesn't seem to quite measure up to your expectancy, don't become discouraged or let doubt creep in. God's law never stops working, and the abundance of life is forever at hand. Your planting and harvesting is not something that goes on during the season of one physical year. It is taking place in your mind every hour of the day and every day of the year and every year of your life. It is always springtime in this garden, always planting time and always harvest time, like certain citrus fruits that always have green leaves, buds, and fruit the year round.

This Thing Called Life didn't give you a garden that

only works part of the time. The garden of life is forever flowering, and so is yours. As you sow, so will you reap. So keep right on sowing even while you reap. Just as nature gave you an increase of seeds from the planting of yesterday, so out of the experiences through which you go and out of the answers to your prayers and thoughts and meditations there comes a new kind of fruit.

Your garden is extended even beyond your own little plot. By and by, wherever you go, you will begin to see the fruit of this planting in other people's lives. Who can say that if there were only enough people planting rightly, this fruit might appear even in far off countries? Who knows but if enough love and understanding were planted in the minds of a few million people who already believe in the garden of God, that the soft winds of heaven might carry these seeds across the ocean and there bury them in the soil of other people's thought until finally they too would reap the same harvest?

The world certainly needs new patterns, new ideas, a new hope and a new faith. The garden of God belongs to no single individual, no particular group of people, to no one religion. The garden of life belongs to everything that lives, and everything that lives lives in it.

As wonderful as this is and ought to be to you and to me, it is not enough to let it rest there. Our joy is increased only through the happiness of others. No one can live by themselves. There is no such thing as an isolated individual. As Alexander Pope said, "We are all parts of one stupendous whole whose body nature is with God the soul." Is it too much to believe that the whole world might become a Garden of Eden in which grow the fruits of love and understanding, of tolerance, of sympathy, and of mutual cooperation?

. . .

Meditation

As you look out on your world in your imagination, see the fields of your experience ripe to the harvest. Feel the presence of love, of harmony, and of successful living, of joy and friendship. It is through quiet meditation and spiritual affirmation that you actually enter into conscious communion with the divine presence that is always around and within you.

Your fields are ready to harvest. Enter into the privilege of communion with your neighbor and with God in the joyful acceptance of the harvest of good that the power greater than you are has created for you.

.

I gratefully acknowledge the divine bounty of life. I am thankful for the harvest of good that love has prepared for me. As I gather the fruits of joy and happiness that nature presses back into my hand, I gladly divide them with others.

I expect the garden of my experience to increase in quiet confidence and peace. I keep myself in constant expectation of good, and forever I pray that I may daily have the privilege and the opportunity of extending this good to others. I sincerely desire to be a blessing to everyone I meet. To every situation I contact, I wish to bring joy, hope, and happiness. I dedicate the garden of my soul to the hope that is within me and to the great longing that is in all people.

How to
SOLVE YOUR PROBLEMS

. . .

Did you ever stop to think that the human mind is the only thing that can comprehend the meaning of life? This means that somewhere back in your mind there is a place where you merge with and are one with the mind of God. There is a place in everyone's life where the original thinker, This Thing Called Life, enters and can, if we will permit it to, guide our thoughts and actions to the solution of all our problems. To find this place, to discover this power, and to understand even in the simplest way how to consciously unify your mind with it would be the greatest thing that could happen to you, or to anyone else.

At first, you may say, "This is too big and too good to be true. How is it possible that such an insignificant person as I am could be hooked up with the mind of God? How could I really call on this power and intelligence for the little things in my life?" It does seem like a big proposition, doesn't it?

Yet, in doing so simple a thing as turning on an electric light, we are using a universal law that flows through our desire. Every advance in science is recognition of this fact. Why should it seem any more strange to think that you are one with the mind of God than it is to know that you live, move, and have your being in a gravitational force that holds everything in place? You are not the force of gravity, but you do use it.

It is fundamental to our belief that the mind of God is the only mind there is, and that because This Thing Called Life has entered into us, we are all using the mind of God whether we know it or not. This is why Moses said that the word—by which he meant the life of God—is not far off, but in your own mouth.

When you say, "There is one life. That life is God. And that life is my life now," you are speaking the truth. When you say, "There is one mind. That mind is the mind of God. And that mind is my mind now," you are speaking the truth. Each of us is an individual personality in this infinite and perfect Mind.

It is the most natural thing in the world to turn to the mind of God for guidance. It is equally natural for divine guidance to come to the one who expects it. You may ask,

"How can I expect an infinite mind to be interested in my little affairs?" Again, let us find an illustration from those natural laws that are so common to us that we accept them as a part of our everyday living.

When you breathe air into your physical lungs, you are breathing the same air that the cat or dog breathes. This air is common to all people, all animals, and all plant life. Nothing can live without it. When you speak of the breath of life, you are speaking of a universal breath. You are speaking of the breath of nature. You are talking about the way This Thing Called Life works in you and in everything.

You don't say that the breath of life is big or little or hard to get at. You don't say, "Why should the breath of life be concerned with so insignificant a person as I?" You take it for granted that it is there and available, and you breathe it. Nothing is big and nothing is little to God. Nothing is hard and nothing is easy. The one power and presence flows through everything, animates everything, manifests itself in everything, and is everything.

The idea that you are one with the mind of God is not an extravagant idea at all. It is a simple statement of a self-evident fact. The intelligence that creates and governs everything is the mind you are using now, just as you breathe a part of a universal breath that everyone uses.

The problem resolves itself into something very simple. The life of God has already entered into you. You had nothing whatsoever to do with this. It is the gift of heaven.

To me, it is the most wonderful thought of all to realize that my life is the gift of This Thing Called Life, that when I awoke to consciousness, it was already here; I am merely using it. This I have accepted all my life without even thinking of how significant it is, without even trying to figure out what it really means. I have always taken it for granted that I am alive and that the life that flows through me is not something I thought up or brought about or created.

This is what Jesus meant when he said, "It is your Creator's good pleasure to give you the realm." He didn't say God is bargaining with you to see whether or not you are worthy to inherit God's realm. God said, "Behold, it is at hand. Enter into it. Learn how to live the more abundant life. Have faith in it."

We are now getting to the place where we can handle it. It is no longer vague and far-off, and it isn't hard to understand. This proposition is not one of going in search after God or of trying to unite your mind with the mind of God, as though there were some great big secret about it. This proposition really is one of acceptance, and even this doesn't call for any great stretch of your imagination, because you have already accepted every other law in nature as commonplace fact in your everyday living.

You are merely going to add to what you already accept, something so important and so far-reaching that it can change your whole life. Out of failure, it can create success. From fear, hope may rise. Sadness and grief can be turned into joy, and unhappiness into a state of mind that makes everything glad.

But you want something more than a theory, no matter how high-sounding it may be. You don't want to leave your theories up in the air where they can't be used for practical purposes. You and I want to know what to do today and tomorrow. Life has put something in us that demands that we live creatively and happily, that we actually get a kick out of life.

We want to bring this dream down to earth. We want hope to pass into realization and ideas into accomplishment. We do so sincerely wish to be led of the Spirit and feel the protecting presence of a power greater than we are to which all things are possible.

Let us, then, see how we should proceed in the fulfillment of our heart's desire. Let us start with this simple proposition: God is really all there is, and this allness includes my own life. I am some part of it. I have an intimate relationship to it. It is right where I am. I can call on it and it will answer.

We are no longer thinking of the mind of God as something far away from us. We are thinking of it in such an intimate way that it really becomes a part of our own mental make-up. Next, we must believe that with God all things are possible. Therefore, anything is possible to us provided that our desires are in line with the universal harmony. And they are always in line with the universal harmony when we desire the same good for others that we hope for ourselves.

If you can say sincerely to yourself, "I wish only that which gives more life to myself and others. I wish only that which is good, constructive, and true," you need no longer worry whether or not God wishes the same thing for you. As a matter of fact, God decreed your good long before you ever came into self-consciousness. This is why the Bible says that before you call, God will answer.

The answer to every problem already exists in the mind of God, and you are in the mind of God. The mind of God is flowing through you this minute. This you must accept, and accept it with gratitude and enthusiasm. Accept it as you would accept the best news you ever heard. And having accepted it, use it.

Your difficulty is not in trying to discover the place divine guidance comes from as much as it is in the simple acceptance that it comes in your own mind, that it is right here. The realm is at hand. Your difficulty will not be what most people think it is, because it resolves itself into this simple thought: If divine guidance is going to work for me, it will have to work through me.

Since my relationship to it is a thing of thought, of faith and conviction, I will have to start by learning to control my thinking in such a way that divine guidance can flow through my mind to the solution of any problem I may have. Therefore, instead of thinking of my problems, I must think of their answer. Instead of saying, "I have a problem and I don't know what to do about it," affirm, "I have an opportunity for self-expression, and God does know what to do with it."

The thing to be certain of is that your mind affirms the answer rather than denies it. You are to affirm that the answer to every problem in your life already exists in the mind of God, that the mind of God is right where you are and is within you now, and since the mind of God must know the answer to every problem, you can know the answers to all the problems in your life.

Keep it as simple as this. Simplicity is the keynote, just a simple, childlike acceptance that God always knows what to do. God never makes mistakes. Affirm, then, that God in you not only knows what to do, but causes you actually to do what is best.

Be willing to take a little time each day for meditation and prayer. Learn to have patience with yourself. Be buoyant, hopeful, and enthusiastic, and try to feel that the gift of life is already made; you are merely accepting it a little at a time. You are accepting as much each day as you can comprehend. Take time out for this. It is the most important single thing you can do.

Then, as you go about the ordinary activities of your life, have a calm inward sense at all times that you are being guided. If thoughts of discouragement or failure come to you, don't fight them too hard. Don't struggle against them, because you do not live by will but through a willingness to comply with the laws of good. Just say to every negative thought that comes into your mind, "Get out! You don't belong to me. You are no part of me."

Having thrown out the negative thought, begin to think in the exact opposite way. For every thought that says "I can't," say, "I can, because God can." For every thought that says "I don't know how," say, "But there is something that does know how." For every thought that says "I am alone, struggling against the world," say, "I am not alone; I am one with God. I am not struggling; I am living a life of faith in partnership with the only power there is."

I know that you are going to have a wonderful experience. There is something in the universe greater than we are, and yet it is the breath of our own breath, the life of our own life. It is a power on which we may call, so close to us that it is nestled within the secret place of the Most High, within our own thought. We know that "they that dwell in the secret place of the Most High shall abide under the shadow of the Almighty."

. . .

Meditation

Prayer and meditation help you to draw closer to the divine presence and to enter into conscious communion with it. Prayer and meditation arrive at the highest point of power and possibility when all doubt and fear are put aside, when you enter into an affirmative acceptance and when you actually believe that God is right where you are. Shut everything else out of the mind for a few moments as you quietly and confidently affirm the divine presence and come actually to believe that God is guiding you. Make this personal to the self.

.

I am bringing all my problems to the altar of faith, and I know that every true desire of my heart will be fulfilled through the power of love. My first desire is that all my thoughts and all my acts will give joy and gladness to everyone around me. I wish the healing power of love to flow through me to everyone.

I now believe that divine intelligence, which is the mind of God, is guiding, guarding, and directing my thoughts and acts.

.

Now, think of some problem in your life that you would like to have solved, and consciously take this problem into your thought, not as a problem, but as though you were receiving the answer, as you continue in your meditation.

.

I believe that God already knows the answer to this problem. Therefore, I am letting go of the problem and I am listening to the answer as though it were sure. The answer to this problem not only exists in the mind of God, but I affirm that it is in my mind now, that something in me does know what to do.

I confidently wait on divine good. I expect to be guided. I joyfully accept this guidance with deep gratitude and with a great feeling of love and closeness to the divine presence that I know fills all space. I am open to new ideas, to new thoughts, new hopes and aspirations. That which so recently seemed a problem no longer exists, because the mind of God, which knows the answer, is quietly flowing through my thought and feeling. A great peace and joy come over me as I accept this answer from the giver of all life.

How to CONQUER A GUILT COMPLEX

. . .

In this chapter, we are going to look at the sense of guilt and failure that seems to harass so many people. It is truly remarkable how much time we spend crying about the mistakes we should have left behind us. Too often, the day in which we live is sandwiched between morbid memories of yesterday and fearful anticipations of tomorrow. Yet each day is a fresh beginning. How wonderful for us to realize the significance of this, one of the great lessons of life.

Of course you have made mistakes, and so have I. Who hasn't? Shouldn't we be as willing to forgive ourselves as to hope that others may forgive us? When Jesus said that you must love your neighbor as yourself, he did not tell you to exclude yourself. You are to think well both of yourself and others.

Jesus rightly said that you cannot think well of yourself unless you think well of others, and you cannot really think well of others until you have first come to think well of yourself.

We should emphasize this thought: "Love your neighbor as yourself." Think of yourself and others as being one in life. Think of that deep self within you as being one with the deep self in everyone else. There is unity in all life, a oneness running through everything that lives, what Lowell called "the thread of the all-sustaining beauty that runs through all and does all unite."

You and I wish to feel that life holds nothing against us, that even though we have made many mistakes, they will no longer affect us when we stop making them. It is never too late to know of the parenthood of God and the community of humankind, never too late to forgive ourselves and others, never too late for a new day to dawn.

But the human mind is a strange mixture of joy and morbidity. We have all had so many negative and unhappy experiences that it seems almost too good to be true to believe that it really is never too late, that right now, in a split second, the sun can dispel the clouds of despair and bring new joy and hope to the heart. Probably one of the greatest lessons we will ever learn is this: All the mistakes of yesterday can be cancelled out now, today, if we permit them to be.

The desert waited a long time to be cultivated with a hand of kindness so that its empty places might blossom, irrigated by the water from the high mountain tops where the everlasting snows of heaven melt down into a liquid, life-giving flow. Yes, the desert waited, but the mountain tops were always there, sublime in their majesty. And the sun was always shining, always giving of its warmth and color. And the natural law of gravity was always causing the water to flow down toward the desert. It was the desert that waited, not the water, not the snow-topped mountain.

On that first day when the water reached the dry and parched desert, new life began to spring within it, new hope. The thorn disappeared and the rose bush blossomed. The cactus was uprooted and the date palm took its place, and the long, hot sands gave way to the green abundance of irrigated lands.

Did the desert look back on its day of unproductivity? I don't think so. Did the mountain top condemn or judge? Did the water complain or the snow refuse to melt? Did the sun withhold its warmth?

Perhaps this is what Jesus meant in his parable about the laborers. He said there was a certain landowner who had a vineyard. Early in the morning, this landowner hired laborers to work for one penny a day. Later in the day, he hired other workers, at the third, the sixth, and the eleventh hour. When evening came, he called the workers all together and each received the same compensation. Naturally some objected to this, but the owner of the vineyard said, "I will give unto this last even as unto you. I will do what I will with my own. Is your eye evil because I am good?"

In this parable, Jesus was likening the vineyard to life, and the laborers to our relationship with life. Those who, early in their experience, come to understand their relationship to the owner of the vineyard and those who discover the laws of life later in the day must all finally reap the same reward. In other words, God gives as fast as we can receive. God and the spiritual realm are timeless. There is no late and no early to This Thing Called Life.

Solomon with all his wisdom knew nothing about electricity, so he was compelled to use a candle. God had not withheld anything from him, because God had already given him all he could take. Thousands of years later, someone discovered electricity, coming in at the eleventh hour as it were.

God was not partial to the one who later discovered electricity. God merely gave Thomas Edison what he was ready to take. To those who accused the owner of the vineyard of being partial, Jesus' answer was, "Is your eye evil because I am good?" Have you less because others possess a good equal to yours? Is there not good enough to go around?

Everyone does not learn the laws of life and the rules of the game of living in the same hour. Is it wrong that we should have the benefits of electricity because Solomon and Moses knew nothing about them? Are the comforts of modern invention evil because antiquity did not enjoy them?

The great lesson is that life delivers itself into our capacity to receive it. The outpouring from the cosmic horn of plenty can only fill the cup that is lifted up toward it. A pail turned on its side cannot be filled with rain from heaven.

The owner of the vineyard represents the love of God and the givingness of the Spirit. The vineyard represents the fruits of life. We are the laborers; the reward, the compensation, is the law of action and reaction that measures to each according to their acts.

The ones who came in at an earlier hour represent those who have gained some slight knowledge of spiritual things before others. They are indeed fortunate. But the ones who came in at the third, the sixth, and the eleventh hours also entered into the realm, and their reward must be equal to those who came first.

If yesterday we did not know that God is love, then yesterday we could not enter into communion with that love. In the hour of recognition, love comes full-orbed into our present experience.

This parable is a lesson of hope. We are all searching. We are all on the pathway of self-discovery. This self-discovery cannot be separated from the discovery of God, because God is the supreme self, the ever-present reality. We have always been living in the mind of God, but we have not realized it. The awakening is not to God, but to humankind.

Don't you think this is a wonderful concept, that the awakening is not to God but to humankind? When the first reaping machine was made, God did not say to its inventor, "It is too late. You have reaped by hand so long that you are condemned to the laborious effort of hand-harvesting forever." The laws of nature wait on our recognition but appear always ready to spring into spontaneous expression for us.

Don't you think that love waits in the same way? But since God can only do for us what we permit God to do through us, don't you think that even God is waiting for our acceptance? According to this parable, our acceptance cannot be only personal. As Jesus pointed out, there is good enough to go around, and we dare not withhold from others that which we desire for ourselves.

Perhaps this is one of the greatest lessons of life. Yet, how carefully Jesus pointed out that this great good we desire will include ourselves through our sharing with others. We dare not withhold this sharing. We should not wait until tomorrow. We must not think it is too late to enter into God's good today.

Let us, then, learn to rejoice in the day in which we live, to find happiness in the commonplace. In this way alone, we exalt the human. In this way alone, we learn to recognize in each other what the hope of the ages has waited so long to discover: that God is really in God's heaven and that this heaven is right where we are; that all is right with God's world and will be right with ours when we know this and act as though it were true.

But first we must learn to live as though it were really God's world. The great teacher has told us that we cannot do this until we first learn to do it on a basis that will not withhold any good from anyone. It is never too late to learn. It is never too late to enter into the divine inheritance that rightfully belongs to us.

. . .

Meditation

There is a golden key to right living. That key is prayer, affirmative prayer. Prayer is our direct line of communion with God. Through affirmative prayer, you learn to clear your mind of negative thoughts, of doubt and fear. This you must do if you are to become aware of the presence of God within and around you. Take this thought as your prayer for today: "God is always with me, and all that I have is God's." Affirm God's presence here and now. Shut every other thought out of the mind as you listen confidently, peacefully, and quietly.

Realizing that you are in an ever-present good and believing that this law of good can bring everything that is desirable into your experience, begin to think and act as though every wrong condition of yesterday were being converted into something new and better. Consciously try to feel that there is nothing in the universe that holds anything against you, and that there is nothing in you that has any resentment against any person or any condition or any thing. Learn to pray affirmatively and to believe in your own prayer.

.

I believe that all the mistakes I ever made are swallowed up in a love, a peace, and a life greater than I am. I surrender all my past mistakes into the keeping of this ever-present, divine and perfect life.

I feel that love is guiding me into kindness and cooperation with life, into a real, deep, and sincere affection for everyone. I turn my whole thought to the belief that today is a fresh beginning, a new start, a joyous adventure on the pathway of an eternal progress. I am trusting love to guide me. I am believing that love guides everyone. I am learning to see the good in everyone and to rejoice in it.

I feel that today is bright with hope and happy with fulfillment. I know that tonight I will sleep in peace. I will awake in joy. I live in the sure knowledge that good alone governs.

. . .

I once met a ten-year-old boy who was brought to me because of continual trouble with his throat. His eyes, too, were somewhat affected. He was getting good medical attention, but in spite of this his throat trouble persisted, and without any apparent physical reason. It was thought that perhaps his problem was an emotional one.

That is just what it turned out to be. His parents were separated. The little boy lived with one parent during the school week and stayed with the other on weekends. He was caught between their emotional conflicts and so became an innocent victim of their bickering.

The solution to the child's unhappy state was really very simple. The parents were advised that if they couldn't get along together, they should at least avoid having any conflict over the child. Their thoughts were actually lodging in the child's emotional nature and upsetting his physical system. Fortunately, they saw the logic of this, and the child straightened out when they straightened out.

There is always a relationship between family conflicts and the physical reaction of children to them. It is sad but true that children are too often innocent victims, and it is no more than just to say that the parents themselves are also victims of their own ignorance, their own bickering, and emotional conflicts. In a very definite sense, we are all victims of our own ignorance. Perhaps Emerson was right when he said that ignorance is the only sin there is. And if so, wisdom is the only solution.

The balance of happiness in the family life is more closely tied in with the emotional strains among its members than most of us realize. By this, I don't mean that many families need be taught to love one another, because in most cases they do. It isn't so much a lack of affection in the family life as it is doing away with mental conflicts between the different members. Most parents love their children and would do anything within their power to help them. So it isn't a question of a lack of interest in the children, but rather a lack of the knowledge that conflict between parents affects the mental and physical well-being of the child.

Each member of the family is an individual, and stern discipline that tries to make them all think and act alike never works out. There is a sacredness about the individual life that begins when the infant is born and never ceases while the child lives. This Thing Called Life has not made any two of us alike. Even in the most intimate group, which is the family, no two people are or should be treated as identical. Someone has truly said that if two people were exactly alike, one would be unnecessary in the scheme of things.

Parents are faced with the problem of maintaining a proper discipline without conflict, free from emotional stress and strain. Most parents already have a right basis for this in a deep affection for their children. They love them and want them to be happy, and of course they want them to be physically well. The family life is one of the most precious things in the world and stands as one of the nearest approaches to the realm of God on earth. It is out of the family life that the community spirit grows and on which our communal well-being depends.

The place to begin, then, is right where we are. We cannot straighten out other people's confusion unless we ourselves are poised. We cannot help others into happiness unless we first become happy. We cannot teach others to get along together unless we first have learned how to get along with them. We have to begin with ourselves.

I once had a wonderful dog who was almost as intelligent as a human. He slept beside my bed, and in the morning when I dressed, he would watch to see what clothes I put on. He knew as well as I did whether I was dressing to go out or to remain at home for the day. If I was dressing to go to the office, he would look sad and depressed, but when he saw me putting on the clothes I wear at home, he would bounce around and bark as though he were anticipating a lot of fun.

Families and children and dogs, they all seem to go together, don't they? They all seem to join in one close unit and common spirit. This dog of mine knew if I were finding fault with him, mentally, just as though I were speaking to him. Children are like this. And we are all children, with just a little more experience. We are all children wanting to be loved, wanting to understand each other, wanting to be appreciated, wanting to have common purposes and common joys, and being willing to share in common trials.

One of the most successful families I have ever known was that of a couple who understood the emotional needs of children and the importance of right mental attitudes in the family life. The father was also a good psychiatrist. There was always confidence in the family. The children were taken into consultation and asked what they thought was best to do. They worked together and thought together as a unit. I have never known an instance where the children were treated with greater individual consideration.

The discipline in this family was good merely because no arbitrary methods were introduced. Everyone was taken into consideration, and the responsibility of each was placed before them in a friendly manner. The children are grown now and have children of their own, and all have become outstanding successes in their own fields. And it all started way back there when they were wee tots playing together.

These parents didn't love their children more than other parents do, but they did understand them better than most. Nine times out of ten, a right explanation to a child is better than all the punishment in the world. Too often, punishment creates an emotional resentment against the parent, while a careful explanation without any criticism instills a cooperative spirit, a feeling that each member is an important part of the family life.

In this particular family, there was also a deep-seated spiritual consciousness. There was a feeling that they all belonged to the family of God. It was as natural for the children to talk about God as it would have been for them to mention the weather. There was nothing studied or peculiar about it. They all took it for granted that God was right there in the family as a loving, protecting presence.

I have seen this work out in dozens of cases, and I have never yet known it to fail. Let's keep it as simple as this. It has been rightly said that the family that prays together stays together. The family that feels the protecting presence of Spirit has a much better chance of being happy than those that do not.

We little realize the sensitiveness of children or how

easy it is for them to be wrongly conditioned early in life. Much of the success or failure in adult life can be traced to wrong family adjustments, to wrong conditioning early in life, to bickering and fault-finding between parents that lodged in the sensitive natures of children, and to the fears and anxieties of parents that are also absorbed by children. In most cases, if the parents are happily adjusted to each other, the children also will be happy.

This is the meaning of what has been called "WE Psychology," where the parents are taught to treat the children as being an important part of the family life. For instance, if the child spills milk on the table, the parent is supposed to say, "We are sorry that we spilled the milk, because it messes the table all up. Let's see if we cannot be careful and keep the table clean and pretty so we can all enjoy it." How much better this is than just finding fault with the child or scolding. We must not forget that it isn't enough for the parents to say, "We are sorry." They must really mean it, because the child is susceptible to unspoken criticism, just as my dog is.

There is no use in stating a problem unless we try to find its answer. The answer to most of the problems of the family life is in the mind of the parent. It doesn't matter how stern a sense of justice there is in the mind of the parent, unless this justice is free from any sense of criticism, it is the criticism that will register in the mind of the child and not the justice. Children feel rather than think, and it is what they feel that they react to. Children are like little mirrors reflecting the thoughts of their parents. They are like little recording instruments automatically reproducing the thoughts of those around them. "As the twig is bent, so the tree will grow."

The most fortunate family group is the one where the parents have faith in This Thing Called Life, where they believe in a power greater than they are, and where they do not hesitate to talk about these things. Our reactions to life are tied in with our spiritual convictions. We cannot escape this, because no matter how adult we may think we are, we are still children in a larger family. Just as a child needs to have confidence in its parent, so you and I need the same confidence in a power greater than we are. Science, psychology, medicine, as much as we need them, are inadequate to meet all the problems of life. It is only as we feel ourselves to be in partnership with life that we can hope to live together in peace and harmony.

You may say, "Are you trying to convert me to your religion?" That is the last thing in the world I wish to do. I am not trying to talk to you about my religion at all. But this I know, the family without a religion is unfortunate. It is not fulfilling its psychological needs, and cannot. And the family that fails to fulfill its psychological and emotional needs will never be a happy unit. This is impossible.

The solution to most family difficulties lies in the need of some kind of spiritual faith, a faith in something bigger than you are, bigger than all of us, but a faith in something that is immediate and accessible, a conviction that there is a living presence everywhere, a presence of good, of peace, and of life. All religions are based on this simple faith, therefore all religions are good.

If there is anything the world needs today, above everything else, it is some kind of a deep-rooted spiritual conviction that must start with the family life. The family that prays together will stay together. The family that has common purposes will be happy. And the children who grow up through such a family background will enter life equipped to meet all the problems that will ever confront them. They are indeed the most fortunate of all.

. . .

Meditation

Believing that God is an actual presence within and around me and in and around each member of my family, I now affirm that my family is a household of God. Each member is deep-rooted in the one divine Spirit of love, of harmony, and of unity. Each desires the good of the other. Here lives tolerance, understanding, and peace. Here lives a unity of thought, purpose, plan, and action. Here lives sympathy and understanding. And here lives the joy of living and the happiness of being together.

There is at all times a deep sense of security and safety, a feeling of comfort and well-being. There is a feeling that we all belong to each other and that we all belong to life itself. We are in partnership with life and with each other. Joining together in mutual confidence, my family lives and moves and has its being in God. All members are individuals within themselves, uniting with all others and joined together in love. There is always a sense of peace, of protection, and of happiness, because this is God's good family here on earth.

How to
HELP THE ALCOHOLIC

. . .

What are we going to do to help those who are alcoholics? First of all, we are not going to condemn them, because we now know that alcoholism is not a disease in itself, but rather it is largely the effect of a mental disease. People are not alcoholics merely because they take a drink. It is when the drink takes them that they become alcoholics. This is called compulsive drinking, which means that their will power or ability to choose for themselves is broken down.

What are alcoholics really doing? They are attempting to escape the realities of life by running away from them. When this situation arises, the drink takes the person, and this is the person we wish to help. We can make normal, happy, useful people out of them only by giving them back to themselves.

Physiological and psychological methods alone have failed to do this. A friend of mine who is a prominent psychiatrist told me that when the problem of alcoholism came up at a convention, the consensus was that it was best handled by a wonderful group of people called Alcoholics Anonymous, also called AA. Since AA has been effective in handling one of our major social problems, we should become familiar with their procedure.

First, those who are alcoholics must reach a place where they frankly admit, "I am in the grip of a force that seems to be greater than I am. I am absolutely inadequate to cope with this situation." This is an honest and open confession, and it takes a sincere person to make it. Pride is put aside and so is prejudice. In recognizing that force, alcoholics do not condemn themselves, and they shouldn't. They condemn the act and not the person. They start with this simple, honest proposition: "This is something in my experience that I am not big enough to handle."

This is the crisis in their experience. Their next step is to say, "There must be a power greater than I am. There must be a presence that holds me close to itself. I must belong to it and be one with it. It can wish only that which is good for me. I must trust it."

Following this confession comes what might be called the great acceptance: "There is a power greater than I am, and I am going to trust it." They are now reaching their hand out and placing it in the hand of God.

They are right to do this, because there is a power greater than all of us. If there were not, we wouldn't be here. Sooner or later, everyone will have to come to the position that Alcoholics Anonymous has come to. We owe a great debt of gratitude to them not only for the good they are doing to those who so particularly need their help, but for what they are doing for all of us. We all need the same confidence, the same faith, and the same trust in life that alcoholics need.

Another step in this procedure, and a very important one, is to learn to trust where we cannot trace, to learn that "for tomorrow and its needs, we need not pray, but make us to do your will, dear God, just for today." Alcoholics cannot say just what they will be doing tomorrow or a week from tomorrow. That is looking too far ahead. So they say, "Just for today, I am guided and guarded by a power greater than myself."

This attitude does not burden us with the needs of tomorrow, but gives us confidence in that only moment in which we can live, this very moment we are living now, here, today. God is right where we are today. Of course God will be there tomorrow and through all the tomorrows that will ever come, but right now, here, today, is the day of our need.

Alcoholics Anonymous does more than this. They say,

"Let us share with each other. Let us share our pain and sorrow, our joy and triumph. Let us help one another." They have hit upon the two fundamental propositions of life: the parenthood of God, and the community of humankind. As the Bible says, "They that love not their neighbor whom they have seen, how can they love God whom they have not seen?" So they encourage each other.

There is no judgment in it, no criticism, no condemnation. It is filled with warmth and color and feeling, with human sympathy and understanding that reveals a deep sense of working with God, trusting God, believing in God, and permitting God to make the gift of life to us. Then, having removed all condemnation, they begin to build confidence and self-assurance on the only solid foundation there can be: the immediate union of God with the individual, the need that we all have for each other. This is parenthood; this is community.

It is said that at the core of every neurosis, there are generally three emotional mental attitudes: a feeling of rejection, of not being wanted; a feeling of guilt and self-condemnation because of this; followed by a sense of insecurity and anxiety. This is not only true of alcoholics, but it is true about many of us.

In removing personal condemnation, alcoholics come to feel that God does not condemn them. God loves them, otherwise God would not have created them. They are, as Emerson said, "dear to the heart of the universe."

Next, the feeling of insecurity is removed by believing there is a power greater than we are on which we may rely. We may trust this power greater than we are. We are being gently guided and guarded and loved by it. Underneath are the everlasting arms.

The wonderful thing is that when condemnation is removed and the sense of security in something greater than we are restores us to self-confidence, we no longer feel insecure. Since we have trust and confidence and again feel secure, we have no anxiety. We are taken care of today, and when tomorrow comes it will only be another today, so we will be taken care of tomorrow.

These are no high-sounding phrases, and they have no subtle or double meaning. They are simple, sincere, personal, and direct, helping us consciously to enter into a partnership with the power and the intelligence that created us and that alone can save us from our own foolishness. This method is simple and easy to follow. It calls for a belief in divine guidance, for a realization of the divine presence right where we are, and for a love for each other withholding judgment. Living together and working together, singing and praying together, creates a community spirit, a field of faith and confidence that is just as real as the wind in our face.

You and I have much to learn from Alcoholics Anonymous and owe gratitude to this organization that is helping so many to overcome the torture of self-inflicted wounds.

There is a lesson here for all of us. We should accept it and realize that here is a principle in the universe that applies to everyone. Don't we all have many habits we would like to overcome? A lack of charity, the thought of unkindness and condemnation for others, the feeling that perhaps we are a little better than they? Doesn't this all have to be swallowed up in the victory of love, the greatest good on earth and the highest gift of heaven?

. . .

Meditation

The Spirit within me is wisdom, power, joy, and peace. In this Spirit I am secure. I am safe because I am one with God. Therefore, I have an enthusiastic joy in living, a quiet confidence and strength, because I know that I live, move, and have my being in divine life and love.

I am not running away from anything. I am not seeking to avoid anything. I am not afraid of anything. I am one with all life, one with all people, one with all good. I am able to meet every situation in joy, in peace, and with confidence. I feel no judgment, no sense of uncertainty, no feeling of shame, no sense of remorse. I sense that I am wanted, needed, loved, and accepted by life. I am part of it, and I feel myself whole, strong, and self-reliant in it.

There is a power greater than I am governing, guiding, sustaining me. I feel safe in the protecting presence of this divine power. I recognize the same Spirit in all people, in all events, and in every situation. I move with ease and calm confidence because I first have confidence in God, the power greater than I am, which is flowing through me. The Spirit in which I live and the life that flows through me stimulates my every thought and act to joyful, happy, and successful accomplishment.

How to
FIND YOUR GOOD

. . .

This is the story of a young woman who proved in her own experience that there is one divine presence in everything and in everyone. This is the story of a young school teacher who learned how to solve her problems through meditation and prayer.

When she came to me, she had just been told that she was to take charge of a class where discipline had been difficult to maintain. As she contemplated this, she was very much afraid that she might even suffer bodily harm, because she was a small woman and her students were all husky teenagers. But she did have a deep and sincere faith in the law of good, and I want to tell you how she used this law and how it definitely worked, because it was one of the most interesting experiences I have ever known about.

This teacher already believed in the availability of divine power but wasn't quite sure she knew how to use it. I explained to her that faith operates like a law, that it really can be a fact in human experience, and that the law of good can actually be used for definite purposes. While she had already accepted this in theory, she hadn't quite realized that affirmative prayer can actually unify things and people. She was in the position that many find themselves in, because certainly we all believe in God, we all believe in faith and prayer, and we all believe in the power greater than we are. Adding this all up together is what we mean by This Thing Called Life.

Yes, we do believe in the law of good. The question is, are we using what we believe or is it merely a good and beautiful theory, the use of which is to be put off to an indefinite future? The question comes right down to this: Do we believe that God is an ever-present help in the time of trouble? The answer will be "Yes" nine times out of ten.

But too often, a definite way to use this law of good is vague in our minds. This is because we haven't yet learned that spiritual laws, like physical laws, are great, silent forces in our lives. We haven't quite realized what Jesus meant in most of his parables when he was likening the laws of nature to the laws of Mind and Spirit, to those great, invisible and silent forces that govern everything.

This was what I explained to her. And so we started out

with this simple proposition: There is one presence flowing through everything and everyone. Just as there is a law of gravitation that must hold each one of her students in the physical place where they sit or stand, so there is one unifying law of good that works in exactly the same way, binding them all together in one unity of purpose. This is what Jesus tried to show in his parables, and this was the basis for the teacher's affirmative prayer.

Affirmative prayer is more than a belief in divine power. Affirmative prayer actually uses divine power—the same power that Jesus used in all those wonderful things he did and the power he told us we could use—for definite purposes. It was because this power was so real to Jesus, so present with him in his mind, so completely accepted by him, that he used it in such a magnificent manner. It wasn't something vague and indefinite to him. He used it in the only way and place that it can be used: in his own mind and thinking, through his own faith and acceptance.

This is what I directed the teacher to do. She seemed to grasp the situation and understand the significance of the thought that spiritual power can actually be used for definite purposes. She was able to make her mind an instrument for the silent forces of love and harmony, of unity and goodwill, which are always available to everyone who believes in them.

Another thing she did, which I think many of us fail to do at times, is that she actually worked at the job. That is, she took time each day to meditate on the thought that the divine presence really is right in her school room. It is in each one of her students. It is flowing through them to her and from her back to them—the presence of harmony and goodwill, the presence of love and understanding and mutual helpfulness.

Let us see exactly how she did this, because it will work in more places than a school room. First of all, she mentally identified herself with the Spirit. This is the starting point. Daily, she meditated on this thought: "I am one with God. I am one with all the life and power and goodness there is. It flows through me to everyone. It flows through me to this whole class."

Next, she mentally identified her students with the same presence, saying something like this: "Each of these students is one with this divine presence, one in it. It is flowing through them to me."

Next, she meditated on the thought that the presence flowing through her to them and flowing from them to her is one presence. There is no resentment in it, there is no antagonism. There is always complete understanding, perfect cooperation, and absolute harmony in this divine presence. In it, we live and move and have our being.

In this way, she was identifying herself and the whole class with one unifying presence in which there is no discord whatsoever. Then something interesting happened. She never once had to exercise any mandatory authority.

It was as though there were a silent force of goodwill operating everywhere in the room. Not only was discipline maintained, but her students respected, admired, and actually came to love her. They brought many of their personal problems to her. They became friends in a cooperative endeavor. In a certain sense—and I think in a real sense—they became her children in a household of God. And it worked.

The old saying that the proof of the pudding is in the eating is simple but true. This is what Jesus meant when he said, "These signs shall follow them that believe." The teacher certainly needed a sign, and it certainly followed. There is no doubt that she was using a law of good for a constructive and wonderful purpose, and there isn't any doubt that it worked.

Let's not leave this example up in the air and say, "Oh well, she had a faith that I don't possess" or "She knew some great secret that I don't understand" or "Someone else with great spiritual power was helping her." This is merely begging the question and delaying the good that might come to all of us if we would let it. It wouldn't matter whether it was a school room or a business or a home, because we are talking about a principle, a spiritual law, something that is just as real and natural as any other law in life. Above and beyond everything else, we are talking about the availability of the power of good and the conscious use of it in the meeting of every problem that confronts us.

It stands to reason that the intelligence that governs

everything and the law that controls everything must provide a way through which people may live in peace and harmony, in happiness and in joy together. If enough people should use this law of good, a great change would come over the whole world. Is it too much for us to believe that finally love, cooperation, and harmony would dominate people's thoughts? Isn't this what Mahatma Ghandi meant when he spoke about that silent soul force he believed would ultimately govern everything in harmony?

Where would we begin to use this wonderful law? Let's think about this for a moment. Where is the first place you and I could begin to use it unless it were in our own minds, in our own thinking, in our own personal prayers and meditations, in our individual faith? Life has made us all individuals while at the same time uniting us all spiritually. Since we are individuals, we have to begin right at home, and this is exactly what we ought to do.

We should take time each day to identify ourselves with the divine presence, not just as a beautiful theory or an abstract principle, but as a concrete fact, as something so definite and intimately associated with the self that each can say honestly, in simplicity and with sincerity, "I, too, am a part of this great whole. I, too, am some part of this one life. I, too, live and move and have my being in God."

Surely, this is the starting point. As we gain confidence, after having first gotten rid of fear, discord, and unhappiness from our minds, we are now ready to help others, to move out into the situations around us with confidence, with the complete assurance that we are in partnership with something greater than we are—an intelligent and loving presence, a wise counselor, and a sure guide.

First of all, there must be a self-healing, because we cannot carry out confusion to the confusion of others and hope to help them. A distraught mind cannot calm another person who is disturbed, and fear added to fear will not produce faith. There must be a seeing eye if the blind are to be led. You and I have to begin by opening our own spiritual eyes, by removing all fear from our own thought. We must learn to live in faith, in harmony, and in unity with others, and then the miracle of life and love automatically transpires.

We are all looking for this miracle, this *something* deep within us, put there by a power greater than we are that knows the miracle can take place. Hope and desire surge within all of us. The very fact that this is so is evidence enough that life intends us to be whole, to be happy, to be complete. To doubt this would be not only to doubt divine providence, but it would really be a denial of life itself.

Let us begin, then, with the self and do everything we can to adjust our own personal lives to harmony. Let us begin by generating such conviction and faith within our own thinking, such happiness and contentment at the center of our being, that it becomes contagious.

Personal atmospheres are very real, and everyone feels

them. Everyone is looking for some sign that the realm of good is really at hand, that it isn't a dream or a fancy. Everyone is looking for a sign from heaven. Let us remember, then, the words of Jesus: "It is neither lo here, nor lo there, for behold, the realm of God is within you." It is to this heaven within that we must look if we wish to help ourselves and others.

. . .

Meditation

The purpose of affirmative prayer and meditation is to unite your mind with the divine presence, to identify yourself with This Thing Called Life, with the power greater than you are and with the law of good. As you practice your meditation for today, take this thought: "And in whatsoever house you enter, first say 'peace be to this house'." Realize that the house you enter means everywhere you go and the occupants of this house represent everyone you meet. Practice your meditation with calm but buoyant confidence and with a deep sense of peace and quiet contentment.

.

Peace is the power in the heart of God. I recognize this peace in which I live as being closer to me than my very breath, nearer than my hands and feet. There is a calm and a peace at the center of my being and at the center of everyone's being. There is a confidence and a joy at the center of everything. It is this peace, this joy, and this confidence that I meet in every person and in every situation. I bring peace to everything I contact. I bring joy to everyone I meet. And my peace and joy makes their peace joyful.

There is a law of good governing my life that automatically draws me to people and circumstances that make life full, complete, and happy. This happiness I bring to others, and this same happiness I receive from them. It is my desire that everything I do, say, and think will bless everyone and everything I contact, and even as I desire this blessing for others, I receive it back into myself.

To the presence that knows all things and that can do all things be glory and honor, dominion and power, both now and forever. Amen.

How to
INCREASE YOUR GOOD

. . .

If you could show how to make two blades of grass grow where only one had grown before, you would be adding to the wealth of the world. If you could show someone how to increase their good, you would be adding a great deal to their prosperity and happiness.

One of our leading universities has done something very much like this. They planted two plots of grain under equal circumstances, in the same soil, sun, air, and fertilizer, and the same care. A group of people were chosen to praise one plot of grain and condemn the other. The plot of grain that was praised and blessed showed much more vitality and life than the one blamed. The researchers were satisfied that a definite principle is involved. Is this any different from you and me praying for each other or blessing each other? Of course not!

You will remember that Jesus blessed the bread before he multiplied it, and you will also remember that in a certain incident when Jesus and his disciples were walking down the roadside, they came to a fig tree that bore no fruit. Jesus condemned the tree, saying that it would bear no fruit from then on, because it was unproductive. A short time later when he and his disciples returned, they found the fig tree had withered away.

How many or us are blessing our physical bodies or our financial affairs? How many of us are blessing our friendships and our social relations? How many of us bless everything we do and all those whom we contact?

What a wonderful thing to realize that there is such a power of blessing, that you and I can increase our good through the simple and silent process of loving and blessing everything around us. We should love ourselves because we are God in action. We should love our neighbors because they are God in action.

Love and blessing are identical principles in nature, and if you and I want to increase and multiply such talents as we have, we must do three things: We must use them; we must bless them; and we must expect an increase.

Someone might say, "What an idle sentiment!" Well, what is more practical than being well and happy and successful? It will yet be discovered that the great ideals laid down by Jesus are the most practical things on earth, and it is up to you and me to begin right where we are and prove that Jesus knew what he was talking about. Are we entering into the more abundant life? Are we exercising such faith as we have? Are we living in continual expectancy of being guided into right action? Do we live with enthusiastic hope?

The trouble with the world today is that it is trying to live without God, without hope and without faith. Someone has to begin. Suppose this someone is you and I, just starting right where we are in our little lives and daily affirming that God is all there is, that good must finally triumph, that faith can produce results, and that love is an all-conquering power. Let's not wait for great events or something to happen outside us to change everything. Let's begin today to remold our whole thinking.

This is going to call for faith, perseverance, and fortitude. It is going to call for persistency of effort and certain flexible determination to see the thing through to a final conclusion. Watch yourself carefully for one whole day and see how many times you are making negative statements about yourself, perhaps in as simple a way as by saying, "Nothing comes out right for me." Isn't this condemning your little plot of grain? How can it multiply and increase under condemnation?

Every time you find yourself making a negative statement about yourself, just reverse it using the positive affirmation that things are coming out right, that there is a divine intelligence governing and directing your efforts. Have faith in this intelligence. If there is enough intelligence in a little plot of grain to respond to someone's thought when they bless it, then there is enough intelligence in your affairs to respond to you when you bless them and there is enough intelligence in your body to respond to you when you bless it.

What is more wonderful than this human body that life has given us? Somewhere within you and within me is the builder of this body, and this builder isn't our human thought at all. It is God, the living Spirit. It is this God we should learn to recognize in every action and function of this physical being of ours. We should praise the circulation and bless every organ of our physical being, assuring it that the divine architect, the infinite chemist, the perfect maker of all things, has designed it and knows how to run it.

If there is a principle in life that makes it possible for a group of people to praise a plot of grain and have it respond, then there is a principle in life that responds to us when we bless one another. Let's make it a habit of silently blessing everything we do—ourselves, everyone around us, and all the activities in which we engage. Just as the loaves and fish multiplied when Jesus broke them and blessed them, so will everything we do multiply as we bless it and distribute the good we are receiving to those around us.

You and I are engaged in the most fascinating experiment

we will ever make, the experiment of proving the power of our own faith in good. We should enter into this experiment with joy and thanksgiving, with praise and blessing.

Isn't it wonderful to realize that this power is already within us, that nothing can rob us of it, that it will not depart from us but will eternally grow and expand? There is no limit to its possibility.

Let's start right now, today, and not wait. Let's silently bless and praise our efforts, our physical bodies, all of our affairs, the people around us, and bless the love that goes from us to them, not even wondering if it will return, because life has already ordained that everything moves in circles, and that that which goes out will come back again.

. . .

Meditation

Divine good is forever manifesting itself in my affairs. I desire to do only that which is good and constructive, life-giving and life-expressing. Therefore, I know that I will prosper in everything I do. I know that I exist in limitless possibility and that the infinite good is right where I am and active in my experience. I believe that everything for complete self-expression is now the law of my individual being. New thoughts, new ideas, and new situations are forever unfolding before me. There are new opportunities for self-expression, and for abundant life and love and happiness. This I expect, and this I accept.

How to
LIVE AFFIRMATIVELY

. . .

If you have carefully watched your inward reaction to life—how you are thinking about people and events—you have discovered that a large part of one's thinking is either affirming a greater possibility or denying the very good we all wish to experience.

For instance, when the thought comes to you that you cannot do this or that or something else, or "I haven't the opportunity to express myself," have you trained your mind to say, "But I can do everything that is right because I know there is a power greater than I am that I can depend on"?

If you carefully study the words of Jesus, in his prayers to God and in his instructions to his followers, you will discover that Jesus lived affirmatively. For instance, when he stood before the tomb of Lazarus and his friends were saying, "Lazarus is dead," Jesus lifted up his eyes and his thought to heaven and said, "Lord, I thank you that you have heard me. And I know that you hear me always." Jesus was affirming that God, or life, is right where we are. He was recognizing the divine and giving thanks that God is always with us.

"Lord, I thank you that you have heard me." There was no doubt in this statement. It was a joyful recognition, a hymn of praise, a song of life. It was not a funeral dirge. He didn't say, "Lazarus is dead and there is nothing we can do about it." He turned from death and the tomb. He turned from the weeping and wailing of the family and friends. He turned from the doubts and misgivings of his own followers, who were standing awestruck at the thought of what he was about to do. Jesus turned from the denial of life to the greatest affirmation the human mind can entertain: God is all there is, and God is right where I am. The power of divine life is available here and now. "Lord, I thank you."

Are you and I giving such joyful recognition to the presence of life even in the face of what seems to contradict it? We all, in a certain sense, are standing before the tomb of buried hope, of vanishing faith and lost ambition. We are weeping over what might have been. This was not the method of Jesus. "Lord, I thank you." Here is spontaneous joy, here is glad recognition.

I know there was no doubt in his mind when he said,

"I know that you hear me always. Lord, I thank you that you have heard me." There was a joyful appreciation of the divine presence that was always with him and the divine power that Jesus used as definitely as you and I use other laws of nature. He did not say, "At times, God will hear me, and at other times God will refuse to listen." He did not say, "Divine power is available on certain occasions and not on others." Always it was there; always it was available.

"Lord, I thank you that you have heard me. And I know that you hear me always." There are three definite mental attitudes that Jesus assumed on this historic occasion, when he proved the supremacy of the Spirit in human affairs wherever we are willing to let it be supreme. When he said, "Lord, I thank you that you have heard me," he was recognizing the divine presence, the unity of good, the oneness of God and humankind.

"I thank you that you have heard me. And I know that you hear me always." Jesus first recognized the divine presence and then unified with it. There was no negative statement here, no denial. Just imagine the mental attitude of those who can face any situation, however disastrous it seems to be, and who, out of the joy of their soul, can proclaim with simple, childlike trust, "I thank you that it is not the way it appears to be. I thank you that triumph can come out of defeat and success out of failure, that hope can rise from fear and certainty from doubt."

After having recognized the divine presence and unified

with it, Jesus deliberately turned to the tomb, which held no fear for him, and said, "Lazarus, come forth." This was a command. There was no quivering of the voice, no stammering of the tongue, no stuttering of speech. Jesus knew that he was using the power of life, which always rises triumphant over death. He knew, as he had proclaimed, that the power of God "out of these stones can raise up seed unto Abraham." So he told Lazarus to come forth. And we know the answer. Lazarus did come forth. At the command of life, death was obliterated.

There is another part of this dramatic story that we shouldn't forget. Jesus commanded them to roll away the stone from the tomb. Let's imagine that this stone is a symbol of that which binds us to our limitation. It is a symbol of a door closed to opportunity. It is a symbol of a locked gate. It is a symbol of anything that denies us the privilege of living affirmatively. Have we not all closed the door to faith and hope and expectancy? Have we not shut ourselves in self-imposed prisons where the morning sun cannot enter nor the evening breeze bring cooling draughts to the tired spirit?

How soon our vision fades and disappears unless we have faith! Faith is an affirmative attitude toward life. It is saying "Yes" instead of "No." It is saying "I can" instead of "I cannot." It is saying, "All things are possible" instead of saying, "There is no use" or "What's the use?" or "Why bother even to try?"

You and I are embarked upon the greatest experiment of life from which we believe can come the greatest good. We are trying to see what we can do through affirmative faith, the prayer of acceptance, and the glad recognition of the divine presence and the availability of the law of good in even the smallest things in our lives. Every day, we will be standing before some tomb of despair, weeping by the side of some grave where our desire for better things has been buried, unless our faith brings to us the triumph of the Spirit.

It is amazing how much time we spend in denying the good we so sincerely go in search after. It is amazing how seldom we live affirmatively. The reason for this is not difficult to discover and is as simple as this: We do not know that we are in partnership with a power greater than we are. It is human defeat we are looking at, not spiritual triumph.

There is a story of a soldier who was disarmed on the battlefield while his followers were in full retreat. Spying a broken sword, he seized it and, through his valor, won a glorious victory. He did not bemoan the broken sword, but said to himself, "Here is half a blade, and it has a handle, and that handle is in my hand and I can wield it." He used such tools as he had and, with a great upward swing of affirmative faith, advanced on the enemy and routed the foe.

Always there is some implement at hand. Always there is a handle to every situation. Always there is a fresh courage if we turn from despair. We are like people in a boat, steering dead into the wind until the sail hangs lifeless.

Sometimes our course must be changed slightly so that we may catch the power of the wind, and then the same force that refused to aid us becomes our ally. "'Tis the set of the sail, and not the gale, that determines the way it goes."

We are embarked on a voyage that we trust will carry us into a harbor of contentment. There is no question that our boat sometimes is storm-tossed, the waves seem pretty high and the floods descend. But this boat, which God has given us if we really knew it, is unsinkable. It was fashioned by hands more cunning than ours. The wind is always blowing, and we can always catch a sail full of it if we steer our course rightly.

There is another lesson that we should learn from the affirmative life of Jesus. Jesus was what Emerson called "a jubilant and a beholding soul," always giving praise, always recognizing the divine presence, and always using the law of good that is available to everyone. To faith and to the affirmative life we should add joy and happiness, enthusiasm and expectancy.

All our theories are no good unless they are used, and so we are called on to practice the presence of God, to speak and think and act affirmatively. We know that this faith will be met by a great deal of denial. We know that people will say, "It cannot be done" or "It's too good to be true" or "What's the use in trying?" We know that people will say, "We dare not roll the stone away. What is done is done and we must accept it." But you and I will never get anywhere with our faith if we listen to such conversation, the very presence of which, if we permit it, would crush all hope.

We know that of ourselves we have not the power to roll away that stone. But there is something that does have the power, and it is this something we call *life* that we must believe in. Someone might say, "Teach me the method. Give me the key to this golden possibility. Tell me the secret of it," as though there were some deep and dark mystery about it that only a chosen few can understand. If this were the case, there would be no hope for the average person. No, it is the very simplicity of it that eludes us, the very directness of it that we do not realize.

The key to life is you yourself. The tomb is the dungeon of your own mind. The stone that must be rolled away is the obstruction in your own thought, the denials of life.

You and I, too, have read the philosophies of the ages and poured over the deep meanings of their subtle thoughts, only to turn from most of them in complete bewilderment to the refreshing words of a person like Jesus, whose words were so simple, just a childlike affirmation of life, just a stretching forth of his hand to that invisible presence that evermore enfolded him in its loving embrace. This is why he said that the realm of heaven is like a child. May you and I be as children in our approach to this great mystery of life, this great miracle of love, this great faith that is within us, this great hope of the ages.

. . .

Meditation

The law is always tending to bring into our experience the things we have faith in. Be very simple and direct about this as you lift up your eyes to heaven and say quietly:

.

Believing that the Spirit is right where I am and that the law of God, which is a law of good, is active in my affairs now, I do sincerely and simply affirm that I am one with this good. I believe that this good includes everything right and necessary to my happiness, to my peace, to my mental and physical well-being. I believe that this law of good brings success and happiness to myself and to others.

There is nothing to be afraid of. Joy goes before me and prepares the way. Love guides me to the fulfillment of everything that is good. Peace surrounds me. I rest in quiet contentment, knowing that all the power and all the presence that there is is behind every good purpose that I hold in mind.

It is my desire that I shall bless everyone I contact, that I will bring hope and joy to every situation I meet. It is my desire that I will have sympathy and love for everyone I meet. It is my desire to help every person I contact. It is my desire that I will bless every situation I am in. Joyfully, I wait on the law of good. Gladly, I enter into communion with life, and with a deep sense of gratitude I give thanks.

How to
LIVE THE GOOD LIFE

. . .

Jesus told us not to judge according to appearances when he said there is a perfection at the center of all things. This is what he meant when he said, "Be therefore perfect, even as your Creator in heaven is perfect." This he proclaimed when he said, "It is neither lo here, nor lo there, for behold, the realm of God is within you."

Jesus was speaking to the outer person when he said, "Be perfect." He was actually telling us that we ought to be perfect because the Creator within us already is perfect. The only way we can translate the meaning of these words is to accept them in their simplicity and interpret them as though they actually mean what Jesus said, because Jesus never wasted time in idle talk. The more you study the simplicity of his style, the more you discover that it reached to the very foundation of being itself.

Among all the great teachers of the ages, Jesus had reduced his spiritual philosophy to a few simple, fundamental facts from which he taught and from which he lived. He actually believed that there is a spiritual center within everyone, and that when the intellect, the will, and the feeling make a complete surrender of littleness, fear, and doubt, we will discover something at the center of our own being that is big and adequate and already whole.

This inner center of our being is what is meant by the word *Christ*, the anointed or the illumined. This is why one of the followers of Jesus said that we should put off the old person, which means all our fears and follies, and put on the new person, which is Christ, or "Christ in you, the hope of glory." *Christ* means "God-in-you." It means the divine child at the center of every person's life.

This is indeed the healing Christ. And if Jesus was right, we are both safe and sane when we believe there is a perfection forever established, a realm of God forever at hand, and the possibility of good that is available right now.

But Jesus was more than a great spiritual thinker. He was practical. He was confronted by people who were sick, impoverished, and unhappy, by those who had lost hope and the enthusiasm and joy for living. It was to these common people that he spoke. It was to them that he ministered. It was to them that he talked.

Jesus taught in the fields and out on the desert and as he walked by the wayside. He taught in the crowded street corner and by the shores of the lake. He said if we would let go of fear and doubt, and gain faith, then we should discover something that we had never even dreamed of. We would discover that there is a perfection, a completeness, a wholeness at the innermost center of our being.

Since the teachings of Jesus contain the key to right living, it is well to consider their meaning. In doing this, we should forget all our long arguments and controversies because they are of no importance at all. We should re-read the words of Jesus as though we had never heard them before, start all over again, get a completely fresh outlook. If we do this, we will soon find that the teaching of Jesus was simplicity itself.

Jesus said that God has made you. The divine Spirit is already within you. This is your Creator in your heaven. God desires only your good. The Spirit has already provided a law of good and has given you the use of a power greater than you are.

If you will only learn to live in recognition of this presence and in harmony with this law, then the miracle of life and love will take place and you will find that you are free. This is what Jesus meant when he said, "And you shall know the truth, and the truth shall make you free." Jesus coupled our knowledge of spiritual truth with the thought that there is a law of good that acts on our belief and brings into our experience those things that we believe.

It might be a little strange to say that Jesus was the greatest psychologist who ever lived, but he was. It might seem more strange to say that Jesus told us all about psychosomatic medicine, but he did. And it might seem even more difficult to believe that Jesus actually told us that there is a key to successful living because there is a law of good that we can use. This is what is meant by the healing Christ.

We should realize that Jesus was not talking about any particular time. He was not talking about only himself. Over and over again he said that what he did, we could do also, and that what he was, we may become.

It is exactly as though he were to come among us today and say, "You are poor and sick and weak and unhappy. You don't know how to get along with each other. Problems of human existence are so great that you sit down in the midst of your trouble in despair."

But it is also as though he were proclaiming, "This is all unnecessary. There is a presence within you that is already perfect. You need not worry over your previous mistakes, nor live in anxious anticipation of tomorrow. All you have to do is to learn to live right today. When you do, previous mistakes will be blotted out and your future will be taken care of."

But, he said, before this can happen you must learn to live right today. It is in this moment of time that we are to make the great decision. It is in this day in which we now are living that we must choose what path we are to follow. Will we live in fear or in faith? Will we live in confusion or in the peace that comes from a deep and abiding conviction that there is a power greater than we are, ready, willing, and able to work for us? The outstanding thing in the new spiritual outlook of today is that we are called on to experiment with this power, to invite this presence, and actually to live as though God were present with us right now.

But we should not expect to change our whole mode of thinking in a moment's time. Even Jesus grew in grace with God and humankind. He frequently told his followers that it might take time and effort to bring about the great but desired change. He said, "This kind comes out only by fasting and prayer." What he meant was that sometimes when we are confronted with great difficulties and seem to be surrounded by much confusion and we don't even feel well physically, when we are discouraged and distraught, this kind comes out only by fasting and prayer.

After carefully going over all these teachings of Jesus and listening to his wisdom again, we cannot help but realize that he is really telling us how to change our mode of thinking, how to set up a new polarity in the mind that will attract the good we desire rather than repel it. Jesus seemed to have laid no restriction on the willingness of this power to operate for us other than that everything we do and say and think should be based in a consciousness of love, in a realization that we must become one with others even as we already are one with God. This is why he prayed that they might be one, "even as we are one."

The training of the mind to think differently is simple enough, but I wouldn't say that it is easy. A thing can be simple without being easy. Again, this is where faith must be used, faith in a power greater than we are, based on the firm conviction that we live in a divine presence that wishes only good for us, and that God has intended that everyone should be well and happy and successful. Common sense should teach us that we did not create the universe, nor need we be responsible for the laws of nature. All we can do is to use them.

Perhaps we have been using them wrongly in our ignorance and now we are called on to re-educate our minds, to reform all our thinking, to make a complete and final surrender of all our littleness and fears and doubts and uncertainties to that great, big "something" within us that is calm and certain and sure, that "something" that has never really left its divine realm even though our minds have become so confused, so unhappy, and so filled with fear.

This is the great challenge. It is also the great adventure, the adventure of faith in a power greater than we are, the challenge of a love that abides forever.

. . .

Meditation

Today I expect the more abundant life by keeping my every

thought and expectation open to new experiences, to happier events, to a more complete self-expression. Giving out more love, I know a greater love in return. Sharing with life whatever good things I have, I know life shares with me the good that it possesses. Seeing beauty everywhere, I have a revelation of still more beauty. Seeing joy in everything, I know genuine laughter. More deeply sensing the divine tranquillity in which all things exist, I have a deeper consciousness of peace and security. Through it all, I know that I am in the embrace of a warm, loving presence forever seeking an outlet through me.

How to
USE YOUR POWER

. . .

Did you ever say to yourself, "I wish that I might never again be afraid of anything"? Have you ever met someone who had such a deep calm and peace that you thought, "How I wish that I might be like that person"? Did you ever, in some still moment, feel as though you could almost reach out and touch something that would make you whole, happy, and complete?

I know you have, and I think that nearly everyone has. We are each alike because we are all human beings. You share this feeling with every other person, and you instinctively know that there is something you ought to be able to tune in to that could make everything right, not only for yourself but for others and for the whole world.

It is said that Jesus, walking through the multitudes, diffused a healing power that touched people into wholeness by its divine presence. His command stilled the wind and wave. His knowledge of spiritual law fed the multitude. His consciousness of peace calmed the troubled mind. His love was a healing balm to the sick.

Have you ever asked yourself, "Why can't I perform these same miracles? Why can't I live a life of magic?" I believe everyone has.

We do not know how Jesus acquired his wonderful faith, but he must have had moments of doubt and misgiving just as we all do. He must have experienced uncertainty, just as you and I. But unlike most of us, he triumphed. He walked over the waters of doubt, the waves of confusion, and the tempests of fear.

He said, in effect, "If you wish to do what I am doing, follow the few simple truths I have given you. I have told you that the realm of God is at hand. You do not see it because your eyes are so filled with tears. Your ears are so dulled with confusion that you cannot hear. Your minds are so weighed down with doubt that you cannot understand." So what was Jesus' remedy for all this? Open your spiritual eyes! Listen with the inner ear! Open your mind!

What is it that we are to open our eyes, our ears, and our minds to? What is it that we must see, hear, and understand? It is this: Life flows *into* everything *through* everything. It passes into every human event and translates itself through every human act. If you learn to think of life as flowing through your every action, you will soon discover that the things you give your attention to are quickened with new energy because you are breathing the very essence of being into them.

You can think yourself into being unhappy and depressed, or you can think yourself into being glad. Did it ever occur to you that you can also think yourself into being well? Into being prosperous? That you can think yourself into success? You can, if you believe in the law of life and use it rightly. But you must learn to use it affirmatively. You must learn to identify yourself with your desires.

Just as gravitational force holds physical objects in place, so there is another kind of force that operates on your thinking and tends to bring into your experience those things that you hold in mind. This explains why faith is effective. Faith is an affirmative attitude of mind that uses the creative power of thought constructively. It gives us a key to the teachings of Jesus about prayer.

We can use the laws of nature consciously and decide what we want them to do for us, but we are not these laws; they are greater than we are. We may have implicit confidence in them, though, because we know they will never fail.

We know that when we plant a certain kind of seed, we will get a certain kind of plant. We know that when we mix certain colors together, we will get another color. We do the planting and the mixing, but nature produces the results. If we can keep these simple thoughts in mind and come to realize that the creative power of our thought is a power that we take out of nature rather than put into it, it will be a great help to us.

We are surrounded by a law of Mind that acts on our thought. This is the security of our faith and the answer to prayer.

To Jesus, spiritual laws were just as real as physical ones are to us. He knew that there is a silent, invisible, creative force that acts on us and through us at all times, whether we believe it or not, and his purpose and mission in life was to show us that these laws exist, what they are, how they work, and how to use them in such a way that only good will result.

Jesus never said that it is wrong to be happy. He never intimated that God wishes us to be sick or poor or disconsolate. Quite the reverse. He used spiritual power for every conceivable purpose, for what we call small things as well as big things. He said that everything he did was an example for us to follow, and that if we do, definite signs will follow our own belief, our faith, and our acceptance.

You must become the master of your own thinking. This is the only way you can realize freedom and joy. Therefore, you will have to turn your thoughts away from lack, want, and limitation, and let them dwell on good.

Make yourself do this. Learn to think about what you wish to become.

You are a thinking center in life, and the chief characteristic of the law of life is that it responds to thought. Your slightest thought sets up a vibration in it, sets its creative intelligence in motion, and causes it to create circumstances for you that will correspond to your thought.

If you think of life as always bringing to you everything you need, you will have formed a partnership with the Invisible which will prosper you in everything you do. If you think of the organs and functions of your body as activities of life, then automatically you will benefit physically.

The spiritual gifts that people have so earnestly sought after are not rare things that God has withheld from humankind. Quite the reverse. They are the things that we, in our ignorance, have withheld from ourselves. Life is not vindictive. It is not withholding anything from you.

Every longing and yearning you have ever had, every secret desire of your soul, every constructive ambition you have ever had, is a whispering of this life assuring you that you are one with it. You are a manifestation, a personification of it. You are a center where life, passing through you, becomes definite, distinct, unique, and individual. There is no one else like you in all the universe, and there never will be.

If you will take time daily to sense the presence of life

within you, to believe in it, to accept it, it will not be long before the life that you have known will gradually disappear and something new will be born—a bigger, better and more perfect *you*. You will pass from death into life, from lack and want into greater freedom, from fear into faith. From a sense of being alone, you will pass into the realization of oneness with everything, and you will rejoice in this oneness.

There may be some who think that before they can accept this position, they must become profound philosophers, spiritual sages, or people of such deep scientific knowledge that they stand apart from the rest of the world. This is not true. What the wisest have known is only a little more than you and I know. They cannot answer your questions for you. You will have to answer them for yourself. Even the best person who ever lived could not live for you. You will have to live for yourself.

You do not have to borrow power from anyone. Everyone is some part of God, whether or not they know it or believe it. But we hypnotize ourselves into thinking that we are incomplete and imperfect. We identify ourselves with the fantastic pictures of our morbid dreams, but the ropes that bind us are ropes of sand.

To understand that our faith is operated on by a natural law gives us the key to the situation. But it isn't enough just to believe in a principle. This is only the starting point. Principles have to be used if they are going to produce definite results for us, and whether the principles are physical, mental, or spiritual makes no difference.

It isn't enough to say that faith can do anything, because most people already believe this. What we have to do is not only realize that faith can do things, we have to find out how faith is acquired. And then we have to use it for definite purposes.

To merely state that you believe that God is all there is will not necessarily cause anything to happen. But when you believe that God is all there is, and when you have implicit confidence in the law of good, and when you use this belief for a definite purpose, then something will happen. The reason why it happens is that you are surrounded by a creative power, a creative Mind or a creative principle, whatever you choose to call it. You are surrounded by a creative power that actually does operate on your thinking. This is the key to the whole situation.

Let us, then, learn to make known our requests with thanksgiving and in acceptance. Having done this in that silent communion of our soul with its source, let us believe that the law of good will do the rest.

If we can then come to see that such a law exists and that we are using a power greater than we are, we will at once be relieved of any sense of responsibility about it, as though we had to make the law work. We do not sit around holding thoughts or trying to compel things to happen. As a matter of fact, this would defeat the very purpose we wish to accomplish. We can no more make the law of Mind creative than we can compel an acorn to become an oak. We do not hold thoughts over the acorn, nor do we visualize an oak tree. What we do is plant an acorn and let nature create the oak tree for us.

This invisible force was real to Jesus. He had implicit faith in it. And because he did, all those things that have seemed so miraculous followed. He was a spiritual scientist who had come to understand that there is a universal principle of Mind, a creative intelligence that acted on his faith and conviction. He could tell the paralyzed to get up and walk, turn the water into wine, and multiply the loaves and fish by a process that to him was just as natural as it would be for us to use any of the laws of nature with which we are familiar.

He used a power that all people have, but which few people are aware of. He plainly told his friends that they could do the same thing. Some of his immediate followers did experience the same miraculous signs following their belief, and throughout the ages these signs have followed many people's belief.

You are in a divine partnership with the giver of all life—God, the living Spirit, almighty and ever-present. Therefore, say to yourself quietly, but with deep conviction:

Today I expect the more abundant life by keeping my every thought and expectation open to new experiences, to

*happier events, to a more complete self-expression. ' *
more love, I know a greater love in return. Sh
whatever good things I have, I know life s'
good that it possesses. Seeing beauty eve' -
elation of still more beauty. Seeing ' .now
genuine laughter. More deeply s' .quillity
in which all things exist, I .iousness of
peace and security. Through u .t I am in the
embrace of a warm, loving presenc. seeking an outlet
through me.

. . .

Meditation

*I now accept my divine birthright. I now consciously enter
into my partnership with love, with peace, with joy, with
God. I feel the infinite presence close around me. I feel the
warmth, the color, and the radiance of this presence like a living thing in which I am enveloped.*

*I am no longer afraid of life. A deep and abiding sense
of calm and of poise flows through me. I have faith to believe
that the realm of God is at hand. It is right where I am, here,
now, today, at this moment.*

*I feel that there is a divine law of good that can, will, and
does govern everything. Therefore, I feel that everything in my
life that is constructive, everything in my thought that is life-
giving, is blessed and prospered. It blesses everyone I meet. It
makes glad every situation I find myself in. It brings peace and*

comfort to everyone I contact. I am united with everything in life, in love, in peace and joy. I know that the presence of love and life gently leads me and all others, guiding, guarding, sustaining, upholding, now and forever.

The End

ERNEST SHURTLEFF HOLMES (1887–1960), an ordained Divine Science minister, was founder of a spiritual movement known as Religious Science, a part of the New Thought movement, whose spiritual philosophy is known as Science of Mind. He was the author of *The Science of Mind, Life Is What You Make It,* and numerous other metaphysical books, as well as founder of *Science of Mind* magazine, in continuous publication since 1927.

Newt List is the foremost publisher of updated editions of spiritual classic texts. Newt List titles are edited to provide contemporary language structure and idioms that have evolved since the original manuscript was published. We revise punctuation and capitalizations, and adjust sentence structure when appropriate, as well as update certain words or terms that have since become obscure, as long as those changes do not affect the author's intention or meaning. More valuable for readers today, though, is Newt List's procedure of changing of gender forms. In the time of original publication, these classic books generally used masculine forms when referring to God or humankind. Newt List updates all its books using gender-neutral language, making the ideas in them apply more broadly to all readers.

NewtList.com

56850826R00102

Made in the USA
San Bernardino, CA
15 November 2017